At least I carried on my legacy

Myself in 1955

Being born stateless

A son of an Estonian immigrant searches for his roots

Thomas Virro

Publish: BoD · Books on Demand, Östermalmstorg 1, 114 42 Stockholm,
Sverige, bod@bod.se
Print: Libri Plureos GmbH, Friedensallee 273, 22763 Hamburg,Tyskland
ISBN: 978-91-8097-137-9

In memory of a father, I never knew

Table of Content

BACKGROUND

Being born and grown up as a stateless or involuntary Soviet Russian citizen, completely without knowing it, was a bit of an eye-opener for me. Who was I really, what was I? My sister and I and our father did become Swedish citizens in 1958 when I was 7 years old, but I became aware of it much later. No one told us, I learned about it when I started with my genealogy research. The fact that growing up felt a little different for me, I thought, was due to my upbringing. Estonia had ceased to exist as an independent republic state in 1944 when the Soviet Union annexed the country. Do I have a Russian citizenship today that I am not aware of? When we became Swedish citizens in 1958, how was a possible Soviet Russian citizenship handled? Was it then automatically cancelled?

My research will be an entry point to look at the history from a subjective perspective point of view, how I try to fill the void that has existed inside me all these years.

The book should not be seen solely as a genealogy work, but also what kind of thoughts arose in connection with my research. How was the welcoming of refugees in the past compared with today?

My father came to Sweden in 1947 as an unaccompanied refugee at the age of 19. He had already been out in the war since 1941 or 1942, a little unclear when, but there is no doubt that he was very young.

My mother and her family's arrival were registered in Sweden on July 19, 1944. Mother was 15 years old at the time.

The fact that my thoughts about my origins began to sprout was also due to the fact that we never got any answers from our parents when we were children. Especially my sister, who often asked questions like curious children do about their parents, but the answers my sister got from father was often; "*you'll know when the chickens pee*" and when is it, she asked. "*Never!*" was the short answer, an answer that was often repeated. The mystery thickens with such answers. Would we perhaps be spared? What was hidden from us? Father must have had very strong motives for hiding his past life, both about his childhood and his participation in WWII, something he took with him to the grave.

My memories of when I asked something were more of a troubled look on my father's face (a slightly tormented expression), a very effective method for me not asking any more questions. What had I done wrong when I got that kind of answer, what was wrong with me?

Maybe it was in those situations I got an invitation to follow my father into the closet to get a little spanking on the buttocks with his belt? Or maybe I had just done something mischievous, in general.

From being a very happy, slightly giggling boy, I now began to stiffen from the inside out. It used to be enough for my sister to tickle me from a distance to make me start squirming and giggling. Soon the laughter started to get stuck in my throat instead.

If you look at this in all, it may not be so strange that you start to think about your background and want to try to stitch together your origins. When words like *Never!* are also spoken, you realize that there is a lot to expose if you give yourself the time it can take and has taken.

I also want to point out that I have never been interested in politics or being out to provoke anyone or anything. I just compile what has emerged in my way and experienced.

INTRODUCTION

When I sat in my geography classes in elementary school as a little boy, I was amazed that a whole world could be shown on maps. How could you know where the boundaries were. I grew up with my parents and sister and my world was very limited.

I thought it was very exciting to sit there and think about what other people in those countries were doing at the moment I sat in school and thought about this. Was there anyone living there? I had heard about something called an Iron Curtain that had been erected east of the Baltic Sea and hid the Baltic States. I thought it was a huge physical iron gate.

Since my parents' origins were part of what was behind the curtain and I thought I would never be able to find out what this mysterious area was, I had to put my thoughts aside and try to blend into daily life.

But the mystery grew and I could never completely let go of the thoughts and maybe that's why I started with my genealogy in the 1980s. When the Baltic States became independent again in 1991, I thought it was best to try to get information as soon as possible, you don't know when the curtain will fall again.

Trying to force information is not easy, especially when I do not master the Estonian language.

But I was prepared to give it a try. My first historical excursion was when I was 10 years old and a friend and I went on foot to the other side of the town and tried to get into an abandoned old castle ruin[1]. We tried to dig under the gate when we heard a harsh voice behind us asking if we were looking for the police, we got out of there very quickly and

---

[1] More info and pictures are available at: https://www.slotts-guiden.info/slottdetalj.asp?id=151

never got to know what was on the other side. The fear and respect for the police was great when we were little and to possibly be put into jail for trying to look into the old castle, we were not prepared to risk, especially not as my friend's father was a policeman.

My friend Bengt-Arne lived a couple of stairs away from me and we often played together. Often, we were out in the woods playing where he taught me how to sneak silently by putting my heel down first and then lowering the rest of my foot with the outside first. I thought it was really cool, I felt like an Indian out hunting. We had no weapons to hunt with, only our curiosity.

In the winter we took our skis and skied far into the forest where we made a fire and fixed a spruce bed to sit on and grilled our apples. Those were wonderful times. When we were hunting as children, it was to see some shy animals, but it later led me to hunting for information. I don't know if I'm sneaking in the same way today for information but the excitement is still there. Perhaps it was the curiosity to find out what secrets may be hidden behind the gate that we did not manage to dig ourselves under as children that drove me to research. But in my case, I have crossed the river for water and instead of today with my car just by going to this castle ruin on the other side of the town and try to find out what might be behind the gate, I have searched all over Europe. Talk about a detour. I still don't know what is behind that gate.

My father arrived in Sweden in 1947, so it took him eleven years to become a Swedish citizen and only then could my sister and I become Swedish citizens as well. There were careful investigations carried out at that time. He had been involved in fighting in German uniform against the Bolsheviks.

Perhaps it was this uncertainty about the situation that made my father a little tense and pondered whether he would be extradited to the Soviet Union, because there was a violent involuntary extradition in 1946 in what would come to be known as the Balt extradition, a very traumatic event in Swedish politics.

You can read about this event in the book, The Legionnaires by P.O. Enquist, published in 1968.

Perhaps this event remains in the Swedish soul after all the years with a bad conscience and thus the lax stance that later came to be held on the issue of immigration.

As I have now researched my family's history, many thoughts have arisen about how it was then and how it is now. The changes the societies have undergone is astonishing, not only in Sweden.

From having been societies where order and order had been the obvious thing, even if it was tough for many people, I ask myself if it wasn't better in the past in some respects, not the material ones for everyone of course.

There is no obvious answer to this as the conditions have been so different in the different countries that have affected my family and also for others.

Was there better cohesion within the families unlike today when individualism and the individual's success overshadow everything.

The people I mainly have sought answers about in my family's history and used in my genealogy research have been on my father's side. From there, virtually all my research has been based.

My search has taken me from Sweden to Europe via Estonia and Livonia (the northern part of present-day Latvia and the southern part of

Estonia). When the opportunities for DNA research appeared, it gave me some answers, but the more answers I got, the more questions arose at the same time.

Is it the goal or the journey that becomes the important thing is another question that pops up in my head as well. It is never possible to reach the goal fully as the situation is constantly changing, new people are added with more and more connections to new people.

It is easy to forget all the migrations that have occurred historically. I have felt a bit like a stubborn, perhaps a little foolhardy seeker, but curiosity has led me to some interesting reading where my historical knowledge gaps have been filled in with at least some material.

Since 1721 up until 1918, Russia has had unbroken control over Estonia, Latvia and Lithuania. In the 19th century, distrust began to grow in the Russian Empire and the peasants began to revolt. It escalated in 1905 in an attempt at revolution, a revolution that was put down abruptly and by 1906 the order was restored. However, it resulted in a number of arson attacks, some killings and burnt down estates for the nobles, sparing the animals and the peasants' homes. Things had seriously begun to smoulder in society.

Who was behind and organized the uprisings is not publicly known, it was pointed out that the simple population had started it all on their own initiative.

If some historical sources are to be believed, the organization of the uprisings pointed against the Jewish people. This was strengthened later during the October Revolution in Russia in 1917. Whether this corresponds to reality, I cannot assess or have any views on.

In addition, an uprising, called the Dekabrist movement, started as early as 1825 in Russia. This started by officers of the Russian army.

The outcome of the revolution in 1917, which started as early as 1905, was that the nobility lost their position in the Baltic States and their estates were confiscated. An example of this is the person who I believe to be my grandmother's father, Hans Johan Otto von Rosen (I have no proof of course).

Losing everything can make you see a connection to the Jews and later choose to join an ideology where a lot of responsibility was placed on the Jews.

I see this as a possible motive why Hans von Rosen joined the National Socialist Party in Germany, where he moved after losing everything in Livonia.

It is not difficult to understand this, how would I react myself? The curiosity about the nobility and what it represented made me collect some material about this as well, which I have included in this book.

The thoughts that appeared inside me when I searched for information have sometimes scared me and can be seen by some as forbidden, but I have not shied away from the truth, no matter how unpleasant it may be.

Even though we are a number of billions of people on this planet, we are so different that we cannot live side by side in peace, but do everything we can to annihilate each other in an infinite number of different cruel ways.

The fact that we then call ourselves civilized makes it all the stranger. So, what is it that makes us express our own desires/beliefs as the only prevailing ones that everyone else should follow as the right thing only.

We have divided the earth into different countries with different cultures, religions, political forms of governments, morals, etc. Choosing these directions must be based on the fact that we are fundamentally different and have decided to set our own rules as the only true ones that we want to live by.

Or is it just a way for a few to get others to follow their values, whether they are the right ones or just because a strong person has set up those rules.

The masses don't really care, only they get their share of the pie and have food on the table. Is development on the right track or are we on the way to annihilate ourselves and that it needs a restart for Earth to be built up again?

When you have achieved all the important pillars and you then start to give up on society's needs and the individual grabs for himself and society goes towards anarchy, well, then the downward spiral starts to take off.

Perhaps everything must fall apart so that we can start building society up again[2], when we have a common goal. Of course, not all people on Earth are on the same "level", but if we take Europe as an example.

What does our short visit to Earth mean if we look at it in a slightly broader perspective. Our lives are shorter than a blink of an eye if you look at it from a cosmic perspective. We are just part of a short life cycle that we try to make the best of. Some manage this well while others find it more difficult to take advantage of the opportunity that is only given to us once, right?

If we start at the other end, the day it ends, what happens next?

---

[2] As after WWII

THE GENETIC INHERITANCE

Using DNA tests to find relatives was one way for me to go and I took a number of tests.

When you can search in different databases with the help of these DNA tests and get matches with unknown ancestors, the question becomes how much you can trust these results. DNA doesn't lie in itself, but interpretation can be difficult.

You need to use both DNA and more traditional research to get interesting ideas for who you are, even if it dates back several hundred years and maybe that's exactly the charm of genealogy, you never know what you might find.

More and more details about the origin of DNA with the global overview that follows make the world feel more unified than you might want to see it sometimes. Large-scale migrations have always given rise to new constellations of societies.

But when these large-scale migrations are going on with the involvement of criminal activity as a driving force to get to a new country, well, then it has been completely derailed if you ask me. The abuse that arises with arguments for relocation becomes horrible.

But even this is nothing new. In the southernmost part of Lithuania[3], in the border area between the German and Russian Empires, there was already smuggling of people from the then Russian part to the German part more than 100 years ago. This was organized in a professional way by the Jews who had an extensive activity for this.

---

[3] The so-called Suwalki corridor

Their smuggling could include the entire voyage from the Russian side to Hamburg and other port cities with shipping companies operated in the United States and Canada. There were package prices for the entire trip and the captains of the shipping companies then transported the people further out into the world.

Leaving aside the Jewish merchants and their smuggling activities, the relocations that were carried out were well documented and no one took for granted or could threaten their way into a border crossing? Today, however, the situation looks completely different, at least in Europe.

When you look at the paths that my branch of ancestors came to Europe and Estonia as a starting point for my research, and where both my parents lived before, they fled to Sweden during World War II, you see a movement from Africa eastwards all the way to China, where the track turns up over Mongolia and westwards back towards Europe.

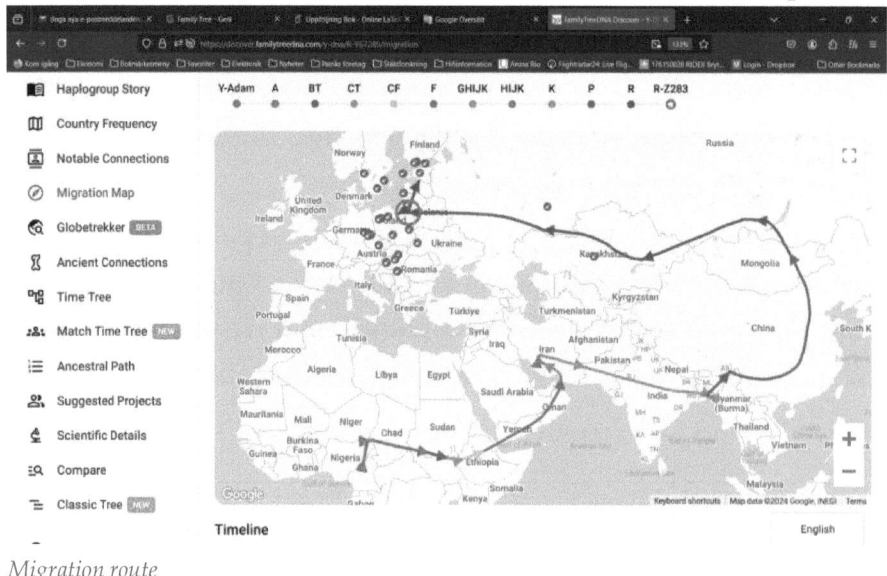

Migration route

As an example, when I happened to end up on the profile Brahma in Geni.com, it turned out that there was a long continuous chain of relationships that coincide with the migration path. The information itself for an individual is not interesting, but only as an example of consistency with the researched migration pathway.

When you look at the map, it is easier to understand why so many DNA hits come from places that are incomprehensible to me, but they are located along the route that the ancestors took.

When you look at the trip, you marvel at this detour as I see it today instead of just having continued north from Africa. Not everyone has followed the line exactly, there is a spread around the intended line.

Latest findings regarding "my" migration path

DNA research is constantly evolving and the current migration route would be this. The connection to Brahma that I hinted at earlier may be due to the fact that that track follows R-M479.

THE GENETIC TRAIN

Following the migration path that my male DNA has taken over the millennia has taken me (my genetic origin) from Africa through Asia into Europe and up north to Estonia. I choose to compare the journey from Africa to embarking on a long train journey with a number of stations along the way where connections from near and far gather for the continued journey towards the present. At all the different stations and connections, the genetic code is mutated from its origin in Africa. We may break bread with each other and learn to like it even if it is unfamiliar to the stomach, but we get used to the new bread and learn to accept the new bread and we adapt to it. Our second offspring may then have a built-in tolerance to the bread and then it is included in our daily bread. We are chiselled out more and more towards the unique individuals we are today. That there are so many different sets of DNAs probably mean that they contain different traits that have evolved over the millennia on the way from Africa and further out into the world.

There must have been a need to adapt and group oneself into different groups where one chose to gather around a common language and the same values. Today there are close to 200 different languages and many use these languages but with slightly different dialects, a small local twist on that. Maybe they wanted not just anyone to understand what they said. Why are there so many different sets? If we are all the same, then we should all have the same set of DNAs, speak the same language. Maybe there is not even any difference between what is somewhat irreverently called male and female?

How important this chiselling was and what it meant for adapting to or conforming to a group of individuals can be debated and debated even extensively. How well would I fit in if I was to move to Africa[4] and settle out in the bush in a hut? Would I be able to cope with a life there? Probably not and I wouldn't be accepted just straight up and down either. Can I then go to the village chief and complain that I am not well received and start accusing the local population of being racists? The fact that I want to sit with the rest of the group at the meal and point to my mouth that I'm hungry should be enough to get full? The fact that I can't handle the language doesn't matter, as long as I can point to my mouth that I want to eat should be enough.

Some people believe that it is irrelevant to hold on to values and that values that a group has developed together over a long period of time are worth zero. We are all equal. If, instead of ensuing the long train journey, genetically, you take a plane directly with your original genetic material (which has been locally developed under its local conditions), can conflicts then develop with the society you land in?

SHORTCUTS

If you look at the road, we humans have walked from Africa to Estonia and Sweden, as in my case, you can see that it has been long with many adaptations along the way. Today, in just a few hours by plane, you can make the same journey to reach Europe, for example.

The time it has taken to have evolved to the present "stage" has been long. For lack of a better word, I use stage. If you look at the map, you can see what a detour it was. Can you make that adjustment in just a few hours or will it be a confrontation between different ways of

---

[4] This is just a theoretical thought experiment with no basis in reality

thinking. The mutations that have taken place have meant that the individual who started in Africa is not the same as today. Man has thought throughout the ages, but has man thought the same thoughts? Hasn't man always had to think about what concerned him in a certain place from a current way of thinking.

From the beginning, we were all hunters and gatherers, it was important to take the opportunity when the opportunity arose. In today's society, we usually don't have to think about collecting food when the opportunity arises. We can go to a store and buy it. Exceptions can be when something is on sale, then instincts take over to take the opportunity. Many people are still collecting, but now money and power.

If you have lived for all generations earlier in one place and then move to an area where people have lived for a number of generations, with the migration route behind them that brought them to this area, can there be collisions in the way of thinking? You bring the hunter-gatherer mentality that has characterized the location you are leaving. Of course, the mindset of that place has also changed, but has it changed to the same extent or direction as someone who has walked over large areas?

Did the same properties have to be developed on completely different plastics or are properties that have been developed if you have lived in one place all the time adapted to this particular place and did adjustments have to be done to move to new places.

The genes look completely different if you test a person in Africa and in Estonia. Why is that? The mutations made over thousands of years should leave their mark, otherwise the genes would be the same for those who left Africa and began the long trek that ended in Europe. There are more hiking routes than the one I describe here.

There is a saying that a shortcut is a late shortcut, that you cannot take shortcuts without consequences. Is that correct?

EPIGENETICS

The fact that siblings can experience an upbringing very differently may have to do with the fact that two siblings do not fully inherit the same characteristics. The different genes to be passed on may have been more or less active on two different occasions. Like the impact of keys on a piano, different tones can be created or different properties developed.

It is also fascinating that at a given moment in a foetus's development; a signal is sent to certain cells that they should initiate a programmed cell death. What was a bodily outgrowth then beginning to be sculpted out as fingers and toes. The genes' execution of tasks can sometimes be random and sometimes very precise. Can it be controlled by the environment or is it only the code that is in the genes that determines this? How controlled are we by the genetic code that we all have variants of?

An example of when things don't go according to plan can be followed in the Russian Tsar Romanov's family where this can happen. The programmed cell death[5] seems to be able to fail when the toes are to be chiselled out. Haemophilia is another genetic variant in this family.

Can one feel any spiritual affinity with previous generations with the same genetic makeup, people you have never met or suspected that they

---

[5] As for the physical hereditary characteristics of the Romanov family, reference can be made to the organizations in which that family has been gathered. During the Tsarist era, these features were state secrets. However, when a child was born at the palace, it was immediately possible to see if it was really a Romanov child. This hereditary trait was syndactyl: the toes of the feet were always grown together. The Romanov family can confirm this.

existed? Are values inherited and that you unconsciously adopt these more or less? Or is each new generation a completely blank page to be filled in based on the current situation alone?

GENETIC CHALLENGES

In today's society, where more and more voices argue that there is no biological sex, it becomes difficult to group people and search for their background if desired. The genes are also irrelevant. But in healthcare, it is not unimportant before an organ transplant, e.g. that the donor and recipient do not differ, is vital so that the organ is not rejected.

But they will probably introduce new subgroups for how to catalogue themselves. Genderless and transgender people will have their own area that disconnects themselves from all the established methods or they will in all their wisdom refer to racist arguments and humanity will have to rethink the laborious DNA sequencing that has mapped the human DNA.

It is interesting when a highly educated researcher stands on TV and begs money to research a special variant of women's heart disease that we currently have no idea how to cure. The difficulty may lie in the fact that you do not know who is a woman or not. Do we have gender as a biologically conditioned concept sometimes and social construction sometimes. If a person changes gender from male to female, the new woman must also be at risk for this mysterious variant of heart disease. If a woman changes gender to male, the risk automatically disappears? A person who identifies as genderless has to be the big winner here. If you are allowed to talk about man and woman at all here, there must be some other risk factors that has not yet been identified for this

26

mysterious variant of heart disease. It is easy to get dizzy in the hat of these gender discussions and it becomes difficult to know what you are really supporting if you donate money.

How they will be able to change the entire DNA sequence with chromosome X and Y is a mystery to me. But they have certainly thought it through in all their wisdom with well-founded arguments.

Maybe it will be a Hen chromosome, maybe you simply choose to abolish X and Y. If you then follow what the English meaning of the word hen is, maybe all the pieces will fall into place. The cackling already exists.

After all, they belong to the human elite and those who do not worship their religion are seen as suspicious, less knowledgeable and racists.

Perhaps a punitive tax should be imposed on certain individuals, i.e. on those of us who do not worship their religion. This tax can then be set aside to maintain their religion and counteract the forces that immigrants from other cultures may display.

NOBILITY (A DYING SOCIAL SYSTEM)

What was the significance of the social system of the old nobility and what does today's social system look like? Inheritance and thus the genetic connection were crucial when it came to inheriting titles and properties. The fact that it has today played out its original role but has been replaced by a new self-imposed class of politicians can be an interesting comparison to make. Perhaps it is only jealousy that speaks in favour of taking from the rich but not giving to the people, but only to themselves, unlike Robin Hood.

Vassal

A vassal was a member of a feudal system, usually with a title of nobility and subject to a king, e.g. The vassal was responsible for protecting the lord militarily in exchange for tax or tribute. By standing up for their master in war, the vassals obtained certain privileges. A common privilege was that the nobility (as well as the clergy) were freedmen, exempt from their own tax liability, especially if they provided a military force for their master's possible needs, armament service.

A vassal could be voluntary or with a good relationship, for example when the children of a king receive different fiefdoms within a kingdom, while the eldest son inherits the father's throne, or as a reward for a great deed against the lord, such as rescue in war. A vassal could also be imposed by an external power, which used the existing local rulers for practical administration, and they were then allowed to retain their position, in return for publicly acknowledging their subservience and paying their tribute, often annually. In case of non-payment, the lord could march in with an army and confiscate the value of the tribute or imprison the vassal, and perhaps vandalize his possession.

The vassal, in turn, could have the privilege of acting as a king within his small kingdom, with the power to rule and collect taxes from the population. In medieval Europe, it was difficult for a king to have control over his territory on his own, so administration was decentralized to local princes who were expected to be loyal and maintain order.

Usually, the throne and vassal were inherited by the eldest son or eldest brother, depending on the kingdom, and in some cases by daughters or husbands.

Disagreements over the appointment of and support for subordinates of vassal states and bishops of the Church gave rise to investiture battles between the Pope and the rulers of several European countries.

A crown vassal is a vassal directly subordinate to the state (the crown).

German nobility

The German nobility was a population group with privileges in society until the state was abolished in 1919, in particular they exercised rule in most of the German territories or at least they played a major role in it. This nobility was often associated with a tradition that dates back thousands of years to the Germanic tribes. From the Middle Ages until 1806, it was closely associated with the Holy Roman Empire ruled by the Roman-German emperors.

Being knighted

The bestowal of titles of nobility began in Germany during the time of Emperor Charles IV by elevating officials (especially lawyers) to the nobility. The oldest known letter of nobility was issued by Emperor Charles IV to Wyker Frosch, scholastic at St. Stephen's Church in Mainz, on September 30, 1360. Families that were not already knights in the Middle Ages, who were only allowed to belong to the nobility in modern times by letters of nobility, are called the letter nobility. In Germany, in the Holy Roman Empire, i.e., until 1806, the nobility was a privilege of the emperor. However, over time, some of the territorial princes also acquired this right.

Inheritance of noble titles and privileges

By far the most common manifestation of the German nobility was the hereditary nobility and the hereditary class associated with it. Exceptions to this were the personal, non-hereditary nobility, especially the official and often also the religious nobility, in which the title of nobility was linked to the person or the respective office. Hereditary nobility and the titles associated with it are typically inherited in the male line in a straight line and equal to the legitimate children of all married people, unless it was a primogenicity title (or firstborn title), which generally applies only to the eldest son. However, in most German states, there were restrictions that a wife of a noble man could not be of less noble birth by birth. The Prussian Land Code of 1794 spoke of a marriage with the right hand. This could only be accomplished by a noble man with women who at least belonged to the upper class. However, the children of a noble man from a marriage on the left Morganatic marriage were not noble nor did they have the right to use their father's noble names and titles. Wives who were not from the hereditary class at birth could also obtain the external rights of the nobility through a marriage in the right hand to a noble man.

Loss of nobility

The nobility could also lose their privileges in the German kingdoms as well as in Austria if a member of the nobility violated the laws or other rules of their class. This so-called loss of nobility, in Austria the removal of the nobility, was the case, for example, in Prussia from 1794 with the introduction of the Prussian General Land Code, and in Bavaria from 1812 with the Penal Code of the Kingdom of Bavaria. The loss of the nobility was first abolished in the German Reich with the legal reform for the establishment of the Reich in 1871, while in Austria it could still be used until 1919. In addition to a number of different types of rule violations; such as engaging in civil trade and membership in a craft guild with concealment of the title of nobility, a violation of the Criminal Code - came into consideration for the loss of nobility.

Those who were punished in this way had to give up their titles of nobility and noble name components, lost their noble status privileges, and were expelled from the nobility for life. The loss of nobility always affected only the person of the condemned, not his family, his wife in the case of a previous marriage, and legitimate children born before the loss of nobility.

Example of loss of nobility

Leopold Alexander von Wartensleben[6] (1745 – 1822)

He was born in 1745 in Berlin and died in 1822 in Breslau. He was a Prussian lieutenant general, commander of Infantry Regiment No. 59, and governor of Erfurt. His parents were the Prussian Lieutenant General Leopold Alexander von Wartensleben and his wife Anne Friederike, née von Kameke.

---

[6] More info and pictures are available at: https://de.wikipedia.org/wiki/Leopold_Alexander_von_Wartensleben

Reichsgraf Leopold Alexander von Wartensleben, II. is your first cousin four times removed's partner's first cousin once removed's husband's second great grandfather.

Du → Flora Eleonora Virro → Maria Adelman → Maria Gustavsdotter Oks → Miina Oks → Rein "Reinhold" Mäggi →
your mother — her mother — her mother — her mother — her father

→ Kustav "Wärawa" Mäggi → Anna Mäggi → Evald Adam von Ungern-Sternberg →
his brother — his daughter — her partner

Ewald Alexander Andreas von Ungern-Sternberg → Pauline* Charlotte von Grüenewaldt →
his father — his sister

Moritz Alexander Theodor von Grünewaldt a. Orrisaar → Elisabeth (Lis) von Grünewaldt → Georg Heinrich Bar. von Schilling →
her son — his daughter — her husband

Margarethe Hildegard Gfin. von Wartensleben →
his mother

Count Alexander Konstantin Hermann Eduard von Wartensleben, Herr auf Schwirsen und Grambow →
her father

Graf Wilhelm Constantin* Moritz Erdmann Gneomar von Wartensleben → Reichsgraf Leopold Alexander von Wartensleben, II.
his father — his father

In 1773 he was appointed captain and company commander of the newly formed infantry regiment von Krockow in Marienburg. With this, Wartensleben participated in the War of the Bavarian Succession and was promoted to major on December 1, 1779. After Frederick Wilhelm II's accession to the throne he was given command of the infantry regiment von Raumer and the Amtshauptmannschaft Ziesar. He was promoted to lieutenant colonel in 1788 and to colonel in 1790.

In 1802, Wartensleben wanted to resign and retire to his estates, but was refused to do so. Instead, in 1803 he was transferred to Erfurt, which had fallen to Prussia in 1802, and he became commander of the newly formed Infantry Regiment No. 59.

Here he was also a member of the Masonic lodge *Carl zu den drei Adlern* and from 1803 to 1806 its Grand Master. In the war against France under Napoleon, his regiment was assigned to the army of the Duke of Brunswick, and in 1806 Wartensleben was given command of the division in the middle of the Battle of Jena and Auerstedt.

It was a catastrophic loss, Wartensleben was injured and his horse was shot. He retreated to Magdeburg with the remnants of the demoralized troops. When the commander-in-chief left the city, he, as the oldest officer, had to stay with Governor von Kleist. Both had a very tense relationship with each other, and Kleist forbade the fortress to be put into a state of defence.

At a meeting the governor announced that he wanted to give up the fortress, and none of the assembled generals objected, the fortifications had not been repaired for decades. Thus, on November 7, 1806, Magdeburg surrendered to the French army under Marshal Michel Ney. Wartensleben was not interned, as he promised not to fight France. So, he remained at his estate Schurgast near Brzeg until the peace treaty. However, the surrender of the Prussian fortresses to the French would have additional consequences: In 1808 the king's cabinet decided to issue martial law. Wartensleben was arrested in 1809. He was interrogated by General Julius von Grawert and in 1809 was sentenced in Königsberg by a court-martial under General Christian Ludwig von Winning in view of his previous behaviour as a soldier, but only to life imprisonment.

The sentence was confirmed by the king and also included the revocation of his rank, all orders and decorations, and a life-long arrest at Fort Prussia near Neisse. The first release from his prison took place in 1810, when he was given permission to remain in the city instead of in the fortress. With the end of Napoleon's reign, an amnesty was issued in 1814. Later that year, Wartensleben was dismissed, he was financially ruined: his estate, which in 1806 had a value of 290,000 Taler, was sold as compensation for the damage caused by the surrender. He had only a pension of 450 Taler, with which he had to live in Breslau until his death in 1822.

Nobility in GDR (German Democratic Republic)

In the Soviet occupation zone, the Prussian Junker was the central ideological enemy. From the land reform in September 1945, the economic basis of the propertied nobility and thus their social leadership role in the countryside was systematically destroyed. Under the slogan "Junker land in peasant hands", the aristocrats' estates were usually confiscated without compensation and they were banished from their homelands. Many fled to West Germany in the following years. Usually, only a few members of the often-sprawling aristocratic families of the GDR remained. It was difficult for them to keep in touch with their Western relatives, nor could they join the aristocratic associations that had been re-established there. Nobles who remained in the GDR were generally suspected of political resistance and were therefore subjected to various forms of harassment.

However, aristocratic titles were also preserved as part of the name in the GDR. Some aristocrats also ended up in prominent positions in the workers' and peasants' state: the SED agitator Karl-Eduard von Schnitzler, the sports official Manfred von Brauchitsch and the researcher Manfred von Ardenne should be mentioned in particular. Some aristocrats loyal to the regime dropped their title, such as the diplomat Ferdinand Thun (Ferdinand Graf von Thun und Hohenstein). It was reported that Walter Ulbricht personally forbade Schnitzler to give up his title of nobility because the head of the SED had attributed a propagandistic value to the aristocratic origin of the journalist: *You must have gone crazy! People should know that they can come to us from everywhere!* – exclaimed Walter Ulbricht to Karl-Eduard von Schnitzler when he suggested that he should abandon his title of nobility.

34

Nobility for money

The money nobility was generally a group of people who because of their wealth, had advanced into social spheres that materially corresponded to those of the former high nobility. The term was used as early as the 1800s for great industrialists whose financial means made it possible for them to live a life similar to that of a Baroque prince. Some of these people were ennobled and are thus counted not only among the money nobility, but also among the historical nobility, e.g. the von Boch, Krupp von Bohlen and Halbach families, von Metzler, von Mumm, von Opel, von Rothschild, von Siemens, von Stumm, Thyssen-Bornemisza de Kászon, etc.

The new nobility

Today, this ancient nobility has been replaced by politicians. The old nobility got their privileges based on various merits, today's privileges are taken without achievements of something significant and beneficial to society.

THE IMPORTANCE OF THE RIGHT BACKGROUND

That the background mattered is shown by this example with Wilhelm I.

Wilhelm I[7] ruled Prussia with the title of regent from 1858 until his death. He was in love with his cousin, the Polish noblewoman Elisa Radziwill[8]. In 1826, William was forced by his father to end the

---

[7] More info and pictures are available at: https://en.wikipedia.org/wiki/Wilhelm_I
[8] More info and pictures are available at: https://en.wikipedia.org/wiki/Elisa_Radziwill

relationship as his father considered it an inappropriate choice as his wife-to-be.

Wilhelm I Ludwig, Emperor of Germany, King of Prussia is your first cousin four times removed's partner's first cousin twice removed's ex-partner's brother.

It is alleged that Elisa had an illegitimate daughter with William who was raised by Joseph and Caroline Kroll, owners of the Kroll Opera in Berlin and the daughter was named Agnes Kroll. She married a Carl Friedrich Ludwig Dettman (known as "Louis") and emigrated to Sydney in 1849. They had a family with three sons and two daughters. Agnes died in 1904. In 1829 William married Princess Augusta, daughter of Grand Duke Karl Friedrich of Saxe-Weimar-Eisenach and Maria Pavlovna, sister of Nicholas I.

There were also rumours that the Radziwill family had bought their title from a Prince Maximillian, something that the church had dug up in its archives. The veracity is difficult to assess, but the church could not approve a marriage between Elisa and William I.

Elisa Radziwill Princess of Prussia is your first cousin four times removed's partner's first cousin twice removed's ex-partner's brother's ex-partner.

When you search in Geni you can find a connection between me and Elisa and also between me and Wilhelm I. Wilhelm's haplogroup is R-M269, the same strain as my grandfather (Johannes Adelman). If you search and try different paths on Geni, you can find connections to most people. However, I do not know what to do with that information. Just a little curiosity, I guess. I also have a cousin in Estonia named Rein Kroll; he got his last name after his stepfather Eduard Voldemar Kroll. On Geni.com you can find a connection between Agnes Kroll and Rein Kroll.

If you look for connections between different people, you can find a lot of connections to different parts of Europe and the rest of the world. It shows how much information has been collected in the various genealogy databases. The question is what happens to that information?

INSIGHT INTO SOME NOBLE FAMILIES

The mentioned families are some of the noble families that have existed in my family's surroundings in one way or another, either as godparents or through intermarriage.

THE VON BRÜSEWITZ FAMILY

Brüsewitz, also Brusewitz, Briswitz, Brysewitz (Brudzewice (Polish)) is the name of an old noble family from Mecklenburg that spread early to Pomerania and Silesia and later to Prussia. The von Brüsewitz family owned many properties and estates in Mecklenburg.

The family was first noted in a document on July 25, 1218 with the knight Alwardus de Brusevitz of Mecklenburg and was particularly numerous in the area around Parchim. Around the year 1460, the Mecklenburg tribe died out.

In Pomerania, a Lutherus de Bruseuitz was first mentioned in 1237, called as a witness in a document by Duke Wartislaw III. The family originally lived on their estates in the Camminer district, where the lineage begins in 1550 with Eggard von Brusewitz at Brendemühle. In the 18th century, the family also settled in the administrative district of Königsberg (Kaliningrad today) and later spread to the Rhineland to Hückeswagen, where the family has a family grave.

The lineage died out in the male lineage in 1819 but continues through female lines. Today, there are still descendants of the Brüsewitz noble family who bear the name.

In East Prussia they were the owners of Lubainen and the Neuguth estate near Osterrode.

Lubainen

Lubajny/Lubainen[9] is a village in the district of Lubainen in northern Poland.

Lubajny is located on the western bank of Drwęca in the western part of the Warmian-Masurian Voivodeship, four kilometres east of the county town of Ostróda (German Osterode) in East Prussia.

In 1775, Lieutenant Carl Gustav von Brüsewitz and his wife, Albertina Louisa Henrietta, née Maiorin, bought from Lieutenant von Witten and his wife Anna Maria, née Hinzmann, the Neugut and Lubainen estates at a price of 13,000 Taler.

---

[9] More info and pictures are available at: https://de.wikipedia.org/wiki/Lubajny

Business activities at Lubainen and Neugut consisted of animal husbandry and a steam brickwork in addition to his military careers.

Animal husbandry

Animal herd at Lubainen

Horses	Cattle	Sheep	Pig
29	97	531	56

Description of the production process in a steam brick factory. Today's production in modern factories is still largely the same.

Production equipment

All equipment in a mechanized brickworks was usually powered by steam engines. After the clay had been extracted in the open-pit mine near the brickworks, it was fed to the crushing plant on a sloping level by means of an elevator. The clay was transported from the swamps to the brickworks, where it was mixed with water and unwanted components such as roots, plant parts and debris were washed out.

The clay was found as clay at the bottom of the swamp. The cleaned clay was then cut, rolled out and pressed into bricks. An elevator was used to transport the damp bricks to the drying room above the ring kiln. After drying, these were fed to the ring oven via an elevator.

More and more players began to manufacture bricks and the competition became tougher, and perhaps this was what drove Hermann Friedrich Wilhelm Brüsewitz to seek out the Baltic States and startup operations there. The von Brüsewitz family had long had brick production on their estates, and the Staarz estate was another example of the steam brickworks described above.

The von Brüsewitz family also had a long line of military personnel. Most of the von Brüsewitz family's men had long military careers, where they enlisted early on as Junker, which can be translated as officer trainees, already at the age of 15.

Maximilian Johannes Alexander Pilar von Pilchau (1859 – 1917)

He[10] was born in 1859 in Vardi, died in 1917 in Tallinn, was a Russian landowner. Reportedly, he was a Russian citizen.

He was the only son of Georg Jakob Pilar von Pilchau and Sophie Clapier de Colongue, landowners at Vardi.

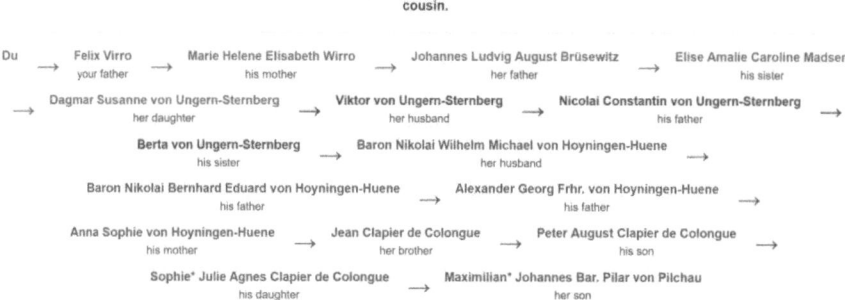

Maximilian* Johannes Bar. Pilar von Pilchau is your first cousin twice removed's husband's aunt's husband's third cousin.

He was unmarried and without offspring, but adopted Hermann von Treskow (born 1907 in Cologne) under the new name Pilar von Treskow. Hermann became the owner of Vardi Manor until 1919. My grandmother's mother lived at Vardi with her husband Johannes Brüsewitz. Max had 2 married sisters.

---

[10] More info and pictures are available at: https://www.geni.com/people/Maximilian-Johannes-Bar-Pilar-von-Pilchau/6000000024670106960

THE VON UNGERN-STERNBERG FAMILY

Roman[11] von Ungern-Sternberg (1886 – 1921)

Roman von Ungern-Sternberg is your first cousin twice removed's husband's second cousin.

Du →	Felix Virro your father →	Marie Helene Elisabeth Wirro his mother →	Johannes Ludvig August Brüsewitz her father →	Elise Amalie Caroline Madsen his sister
→	Dagmar Susanne von Ungern-Sternberg her daughter →	Viktor von Ungern-Sternberg her husband →	Nicolai Constantin von Ungern-Sternberg his father →	
	Freiherr Fredrik Adolf * von Ungern-Sternberg his father →	Friedrich Robert Eginhard von Ungern-Sternberg his brother →		
	Teodor Leonhard Rudolf von Ungern-Sternberg his son →	Roman von Ungern-Sternberg his son		

How the noble Baron von Ungern liberated Mongolia.

Roman von Ungern-Sternberg[12] (1886 - 1921) lived an extraordinary life. An aristocrat with German roots, he embraced Buddhism and liberated Mongolia from Chinese occupation. At the same time, he tried to prevent the Bolsheviks from taking power and creating a Eurasian empire.

There were many people in Europe who looked east for spiritual support, both before and after Baron von Ungern, the Russian writer Leonid Yusevich wrote in his biography of the man. But he was the only one who managed to convert this support into military power.

Roman von Ungern-Sternberg was a Russian nobleman with German roots who spent his last days fighting to re-establish the Russian Empire in Siberia and Mongolia with the support of his Asian horsemen.

He was considered extremely brave and bordering on crazy.

The noble von Ungern-Sternberg family served Russia since the 1870s, although they actually came from Germany. Roman von Ungern,

---

[11] More info and pictures are available at: https://en.wikipedia.org/wiki/Roman_von_Ungern-Sternberg

[12] Source material for Roman von Ungern-Sternberg Roman von Ungern-Sternberg

the youngest descendant of the family, was absolutely convinced that there was no other way for Russia than to remain under the tsarist leadership of the Romanovs forever.

At the same time, however, von Ungern himself was considered to be rebellious. For example, in his youth he was almost expelled from school due to fighting and drinking. But these antics were linked to a deep patriotism.

During World War I, von Ungern fought on the Russian side against Austria-Hungary and the Ottoman Empire. He was wounded five times and received the Russian Order of St. George, the symbol of military heroism.

Yet he also acted erratically during this time - he was in prison for two months due to an attack on another officer. After the February Revolution in 1917, he moved to the Far East.

A Buddhist with a sword

He did not make the decision to move east spontaneously. von Ungern was fascinated by Asian culture and had previously visited the region several times. He was particularly interested in Tibetan Buddhism and the life of the Mongols, Buryats, and other Asian peoples on the borders of Russia. In return, these people also showed von Ungern great respect, especially because of his outstanding riding skills. This mutual respect would be of indescribable benefit to von Ungern during his future military escapades in Mongolia.

He eventually converted to Buddhism, but did not believe in the demand for non-violence. After Vladimir Lenin and the Bolsheviks seized power in 1917, von Ungern swore loyalty to the Romanovs and fought alongside other commanders of the White Army in Siberia against Red Army troops in the civil war.

The Mongol Campaign

In 1921, the imminent defeat of the Whites became evident and the Red Army moved more and more rapidly to the east. von Ungern decided to leave Russia. But he chose a different path than many other commanders in the White Army. Instead of fleeing to Europe, he transformed the Asiatic cavalry unit, composed mainly of local volunteers, into a guerrilla force and crossed the Russo-Mongol border with it.

At that time, Mongolia was occupied by Chinese troops. The Mongol spiritual leader Bogd Khan, lived under house arrest in the capital Urga, now Ulaanbaatar. The Chinese garrison in the city consisted of 7,000 men and exceeded von Ungern's troop strength five times. Despite this, the baron managed to defeat the Chinese occupiers and liberate the city. A short time later, the enemy soldiers were driven out of all of Mongolia.

The last Russian Khan

The Mongols glorified von Ungern. Bogd Khan returned to the head of the country and awarded him the title of Khan, the highest award for a military leader. The baron enjoyed a high reputation in the country and the Mongols called him the god of war because of his victory over the occupiers.

von Ungern, however, was an autocratic leader and ordered the deaths of hundreds of people. According to Russian historian Sergei Kuzmin, about 850 people died on the barons' orders between February and August 1921. Nor did the violent and brutal von Ungern hesitate to condemn its own people to death – often for harmless crimes.

In any case, the baron was never satisfied with just controlling Mongolia. According to historian Stanislav Khatuntsev he wanted to launch a campaign against the West, the source of all revolutions, and to do this use the power of Asia to bring Asian culture and beliefs to all of Eurasia, thereby rebuilding the fallen monarchies.

The fateful end

But the campaign was destined to fail. In May 1921, von Ungern invaded Soviet Russia with 4,000 men. He had speculated that the people of Siberia were dissatisfied with the Bolsheviks and would join his struggle. But that did not happen – the baron's army was defeated. In the end, he was betrayed by his own men and handed over to the Red Army.

von Ungern was executed the same year in Novonikolayevsk, today's Novosibirsk, 2,800 kilometres east of Moscow. Official sources say that he was completely calm during the interrogations and even shortly before his death – as befits a true Buddhist.

Viktor von Ungern-Sternberg (1896 – 1939)

Viktor[13] was married to my grandmother's foster father's niece.

He and Roman had been on the train to the R-M198 station. What happened next is unclear.

---

[13] More info and pictures are available at: https://www.geni.com/people/Viktor-von-Ungern-Sternberg/6000000015908516771

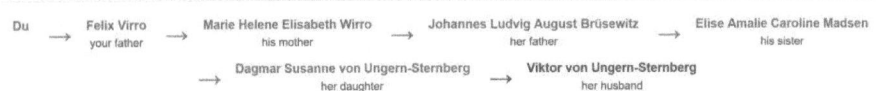

Who has done the test Victor belonged to and how extensive was it? My grandson Lukas, who I tested at the 37-marker level of Y-DNA, also shows the same result, R-M198. In order for Lukas to get my result, we need to expand his test. Which carriage or compartment is unclear. At least until Belarus we have been on the same train, where the track splits into 2 branches where one branch turns off down towards Hungary and the other continues into Poland according to FamilyTreeDNA. Perhaps Viktor's name can give a clue as to which path he took.

Could it be that Viktor did not change trains and thus did not go to Hungary?

COUNT KARL EDUARD VON SIEVERS (1795–1873 IN BERLIN)

Count Karl Eduard von Sievers is your first cousin four times removed's partner's first cousin's wife's father.

He was the owner of the estates (Wilsenhof/Vilzeni) in Livonia and the estates of Rasik/Raasiku and Campen/Cambi in Estonia, outside Tallinn.

At Wilsenhof/Vilzeni Carl Friedrich Wilhelm Brüsewitz was born in 1862. He was, together with the other children listed here, siblings of my grandmother.

Eduard Robert Hermann Brüsewitz was born at Rasik/Raasiku in 1872, Emil August Wilhelm Brüsewitz in 1897 and Marie Julie Amalie Brüsewitz in 1876.

 Dorothea Elisabeth Julie Brüsewitz was born at Campen/Cambi in 1866, Elwine Caroline Wilhelmine Brüsewitz in 1868, Elise Amalie Caroline Brüsewitz in 1870 and Johannes Ludvig August Brüsewitz in 1874.The camp was a so-called support estate to Rasik.

Why Hermann stated that he was a Prussian Landwehrmann when his first son was born in Livonia seems a bit strange since he worked as *Torfstecher* and *Ziegelbrenner*. Does this indicate that he still had a connection to a regiment somewhere in Prussia and that he could be called up if necessary?

Karl von Sievers and his daughter Elisabeth (Lilly) were godparents to Elisabeth Cecilie Karoline Brüsewitz in 1864 and Elise Amalie Caroline Brüsewitz in 1870.

Elisabeth was also godmother to Marie Julie Amalie Brüsewitz in 1876 and Emil August Wilhelm Brüsewitz in 1879.

How the connection was between the von Sievers and Brüsewitz families is unclear to me? I read in a letter that Bodo Brüsewitz wrote to Tiiu Oja at Eesti Ajaloo Arhiiv (EHA) in 2001:

Die Eltern von Johannes Brüsewitz wurden von dem damaligen Gutsbesitzer eingeladen, in alter Freundschaft den Rest ihres Lebens auf seinem Gut zu verbringen.

This means that the parents of the Brüsewitz family were invited by the then landowner of Rasik, von Sievers, to spend the rest of their lives on the estate for the sake of old friendship.

He doesn't write for old and faithful ministry or anything. Where did Bodo (Bodo is Hermann's great-grandson) get that information from? The landowner would then have been Graf von Sievers. Is it hearsay in the same way as Gerda?

When Count Karl Eduard von Sievers died in 1873 in Berlin, the situation probably changed for the Brüsewitz family. The sons later took over the estate and Herrman and his family moved to Wolhynia. However, they were still in Tallinn in 1893 when Hermann's son Johannes married my grandmother's mother.

BARONESS HELENE VON KEYSERLINGK (1876 - ?)

Helene von Keyserlingk was godmother to Werner Friedrich Wilhelm Brüsewitz in 1894.

Alexandra Virginie Helene* Bsse. von Keyserlingk is your first cousin twice removed's husband's first cousin's husband's wife's third cousin.

| Du | → | Felix Virro your father | → | Marie Helene Elisabeth Wirro his mother | → | Johannes Ludvig August Brüsewitz her father | → | Elise Amalie Caroline Madsen his sister |

Dagmar Susanne von Ungern-Sternberg her daughter → Viktor von Ungern-Sternberg her husband → Nicolai Constantin von Ungern-Sternberg his father →

Marie Pauline Renata von Carlsburg his sister → Irmgard von Hoyningen-Huene her daughter → Alexander Gottlieb Ferdinand Baron von Hoyningen Huene her husband

Pauline Wilhelmine von Hoyningen-Huene his wife → Julie Charlotte Wilhelmine Esperance Elisabeth von Essen her mother →

Juliane Wilhelmine von Dellingshausen her mother → Marie Louise* Julie Theresia von Kleist her mother → Franz Friedrich Gotthard (Franz) von Keyserlingk her brother

Wilhelm* Johann Bar. von Keyserlingk his son → Bar. Heinrich Hermann Alfred* von Keyserlingk his son →

Alexandra Virginie Helene* Bsse. von Keyserlingk his daughter

I have not been able to find any traces of Werner.

AUGUST VON SCHULMAN (1886 – 1945)

August[14] was godfather to Voldemar August Brüsewitz in 1907, brother of his grandmother.

August° Detlef von Schulmann is your first cousin twice removed's husband's first cousin once removed's ex-wife's daughter's husband's brother.

Du	→	Felix Virro (your father)	→	Marie Helene Elisabeth Wirro (his mother)	→	Johannes Ludvig August Brüsewitz (her father)	→	Elise Amalie Caroline Madsen (his sister)
→	Dagmar Susanne von Ungern-Sternberg (her daughter)	→	Viktor von Ungern-Sternberg (her husband)	→	Nicolai Constantin von Ungern-Sternberg (his father)	→
Freiherr Fredrik Adolf ° von Ungern-Sternberg (his father)	→	Friedrich Robert Eginhard von Ungern-Sternberg (his brother)	→
Teodor Leonhard Rudolf von Ungern-Sternberg (his son)	→	Sofie° Charlotte Freiin von Wimpffen (his ex-wife)	→
Isabella° Margaretha Bsse. von Hoyningen-Huene (her daughter)	→	Otto° Wilhelm von Schulmann (her husband)	→	August° Detlef von Schulmann (his brother)

ALEXANDER NIKOLAI VON GLEHN (1841 – 1923)

He[15] was born in 1841 and died in 1923 in Brazil

Landlord at Jelgimeggi/Jälgimäe -

He was a Baltic German landowner and public figure, best known for being the founder of the city of Nõmme (now part of Tallinn). Governor of Estonia, Russia.

Alexander Nikolai° von Glehn is your first cousin twice removed's husband's second cousin's husband's first cousin's husband's father.

Du	→	Felix Virro (your father)	→	Marie Helene Elisabeth Wirro (his mother)	→	Johannes Ludvig August Brüsewitz (her father)	→	Elise Amalie Caroline Madsen (his sister)
→	Dagmar Susanne von Ungern-Sternberg (her daughter)	→	Viktor von Ungern-Sternberg (her husband)	→	Nicolai Constantin von Ungern-Sternberg (his father)	→
Freiherr Fredrik Adolf ° von Ungern-Sternberg (his father)	→	Maximilian Woldemar von Ungern-Sternberg (his brother)	→
Alexandra Natalie von Hoyningen-Huene (his daughter)	→	Agnes Pauline Natalie von Baranoff (her daughter)	→	Alexei (Ali) Gregor Alexander von Baranoff, a. Sonorm (her husband)	→
Julie Marie Helene von Baranoff (his mother)	→	Karoline Christine Marie von Helffreich (her sister)	→	Elisabeth Auguste Charlotte von Glehn (her daughter)	→
Manfred Nikolai von Glehn (her husband)	→	Alexander Nikolai° von Glehn (his father)

---

[14] More info and pictures are available at: https://www.geni.com/people/August-Detlef-von-Schulmann/6000000003083216284

[15] More info and pictures are available at: https://en.wikipedia.org/wiki/Nikolai_von_Glehn

Emil August Heinrich Brüsewitz was born at Jelgimeggi/Jälgimäe in 1896, Johannes Oswald Theodor Brüsewitz in 1899 and Bertha Helene Alide Brüsewitz in 1902.

Johannes had married Marri in 1893, when she was probably a house-keeper at Vardi for Max Pilar von Pilchau.

LIBERAL WINDS ARE BLOWING IN RUSSIA

That the old order in Russia was beginning to be threatened was shown in what came to be called the Dekabrists' rebellion, an unsuccessful attempt at a palace revolution. The term *Dekabrist* (Russian: декабрист) comes from the Russian word *dekabr* (Russian: декабрь) which means *December*.

The Dekabrist Rebellion[16]

It took place in Russia in December 1825, after[17] the sudden death of Emperor Alexander I.

Aleksander I Pavlovich Romanov, Emperor and Autocrat of All the Russias is your first cousin twice removed's husband's third great uncle's ex-wife's grandson's wife's mother's ex-partner.

Du →	Felix Virro your father →	Marie Helene Elisabeth Wirro his mother →	Johannes Ludvig August Brüsewitz her father →	Elise Amalie Caroline Madsen his sister
→	Dagmar Susanne von Ungern-Sternberg her daughter →	Viktor von Ungern-Sternberg her husband →	Nicolai Constantin von Ungern-Sternberg his father →	
Anna Auguste * Elisabeth von Ungern-Sternberg his mother →	Johanna Carolina von Ungern-Sternberg her mother →	Anna Charlotta Posse af Säby her mother →		
Moritz Posse af Säby her brother →	Euphrosine Ulrike von Liphart his ex-wife →	Natalia Ivanovna Goncharova her daughter →	Иван Николаевич Гончаров her son →	
Мария Ивановна Гончарова his wife →	Sophia Sergievna Мещерская her mother →			
Aleksander I Pavlovich Romanov, Emperor and Autocrat of All the Russias her ex-partner				

Alexander's heir, Konstantin, had declined the inheritance, he was unknown to the court, so his younger brother Nicholas ascended the throne as Emperor Nicholas I. While part of the army had sworn loyalty to Nicholas, a force of about 3,000 soldiers attempted to stage a military coup in favour of Konstantin.

Although weakened by disagreement among their leaders, the rebels confronted the Loyalists outside the Senate building with a large crowd. In the confusion, the emperor's envoy, Mikhail Miloradovich, was assassinated[18].

Count Mikhail Andreyevich Miloradovich is your first cousin twice removed's husband's second cousin's husband's ex-wife's grandfather's ex-partner's ex-partner.

It turns out that there is a connection between us. Johannes Ludwig August Brüsewitz is probably my grandmother's stepfather and not the biological father mentioned here. There is another person who I believe was her biological father.

Eventually, the Loyalists opened fire with heavy artillery, which dispersed the rebels. Many were subsequently sentenced to hanging, imprisonment or exile to Siberia. The conspirators became known as Dekabrists.

---

[18] More info and pictures are available at: https://en.wikipedia.org/wiki/Mikhail_Miloradovich

Initially, many officers were encouraged by Tsar Alexander I's early liberal reforms of Russian society and politics. Liberalism was encouraged at the official level, which created high expectations during the period of rapprochement between Napoleon and Alexander.

The great advocate of reforms in Alexander's regime was Count Mikhail Mikhailovich Speransky[19].

He is seen as the father of Russian liberalism. During his first years in the regime, Speransky helped to inspire the organization of the Ministry of the Interior, reform ecclesiastical education, and to strengthen the role of the government in the country's economic development. Speransky's role increased greatly in 1808. Since then, until 1812, when they feared him as a liberal, similar to Napoleon and his invasion, Speransky developed plans for the reorganization of Russia's government in exile.

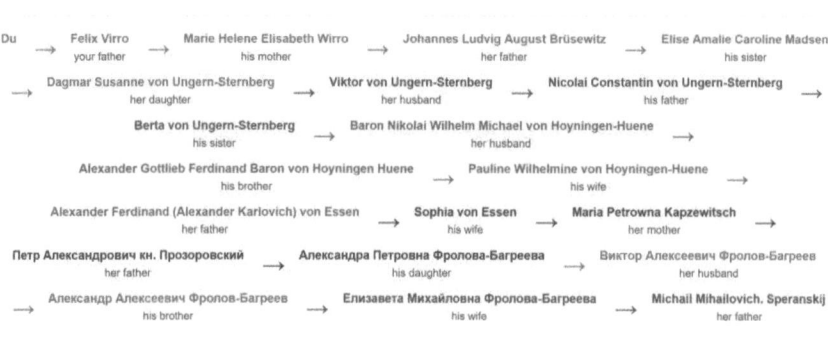

Michail Mihailovich. Speranskij is your first cousin twice removed's husband's aunt's husband's brother's wife's father's wife's aunt's husband's brother's wife's father.

---

[19] More info and pictures are available at: https://en.wikipedia.org/wiki/Mikhail_Speransky

On his return from exile in 1819, he was appointed governor of Siberia, with the task of reforming the local government. In 1818, the Tsar asked Count Nikolay Nikolayevich Novosiltsev to draft a constitution.

However, internal and external unrest, which the tsar believed stemmed from political liberalization, led to a series of repressions and a return to a previous government advocating restraint and conservatism. In the meantime, the experiences of the Napoleonic Wars and the realization of the suffering of peasant soldiers resulted in Dekabrist officers and sympathizers being attracted to reform changes in society.

In 1816, several officers of the Imperial Russian Guard founded a society known as the Salvation Covenant, or as the Faithful and True Sons of the Fatherland.

The time of the Dekabrists in Siberia

After the rebellion was put down, in 1826 the first group of Dekabrist prisoners began their exodus towards Siberia. Among this group were Prince Trubetskoi, Prince Obolensky, Peter and Andrei Borisov, Prince Volkonsky and Artamon Muraviev, all on their way to the mines of Nerchinsk.

The journey east was fraught with difficulties, but for some it offered refreshing changes in landscape and people after prison. Dekabrist Nikolay Vasilyevich Basargin felt unwell when he set off from St. Petersburg, but he recovered during the journey; his memoirs depict the journey to Siberia in a cheerful light, full of praise for the public and commanding landscapes. Not all Dekabrists could identify with the positive experience of Basargin. Because of their lower social status, the soldier-Dekabrists experienced the emperor's revenge to the fullest.

Judged by a court-martial, many of these peasant people received thousands of lashes. Those who survived went to Siberia on foot, chained up with common criminals. Fifteen of the 124 Dekabrists were convicted of state crimes by the Supreme Criminal Court and sentenced to exile. These men were sent directly to isolated places such as Berezov, Narym, Surgut, Pelym, Irkutsk, Yakutsk and Viliuisk.

Few Russians inhabited these places. Of all those exiled, the largest group of prisoners were sent to Chita, Zabaykalsky Krai, transferred three years later to Petrovsky Zavod, near Nerchinsk. This group, doomed to hard labour, included their main leaders of the Dekabrist movement as well as members of the United Slavs.

Most of the Dekabrists left Petrovsky Zavod between 1835 and 1837 and settled in or near Irkutsk, Minusinsk, Kurgan, Tobolski, Turinsk, and Yalutorovsk. The Dekabrists who had already lived in or visited Siberia, such as Dimitri Zavalishin, flourished when they left Petrovsky Zavods borders, but most found it physically exhausting and more psychologically nervous than prison life.

Dekabrists in Chita, Zabaykalsky Krai, 1885

The Siberian population greeted the Dekabrists with great hospitality. The natives played a central role in keeping lines of communication open between Dekabrists, friends, and relatives. Most merchants and government employees were also sympathetic. To the masses, the Dekabrists were the exulant officers who had refused to take the oath to Nicholas I. Overall, the indigenous Siberian population greatly respected the Dekabrists and were extremely hospitable in their reception of them.

It has turned out that there is a DNA connection between Chita in Russia and my family in Estonia through this man.

▣ 1 Step Match

Name: **Mr. Mikhail Arkhangelskii**
Earliest Known Ancestor: **Vladimir Arkhangelskii, b. 1938**
Marker Location: **Chita, Zabaykalsky Krai, Russia**

michael.archangelski@gmail.com

YDNA Coupling

The Dekabrist leader Prince Sergei Volkonsky[20] returned to St. Petersburg after 30 years of his exile had elapsed, although his titles and land remained under royal ownership.

Other exiles preferred to remain in Siberia after their sentences had been served, preferring its relative freedom to the suffocating intrigues of Moscow and St. Petersburg, and after years of exile there was little for them to return to. Many Dekabrists thrived in exile and eventually became landowners and farmers.

Maj. Gen. Prince Sergei Grigorievich Volkonsky is your first cousin's partner's first cousin once removed's niece's ex-husband's second great grandfather.

In later years, they became idols of the populist movement of the 1860s and 1870s, as the Dekabrist' advocacy of reforms (including the

---

[20] More info and pictures are available at: https://en.wikipedia.org/wiki/Sergey_Volkonsky

abolition of serfdom) earned them many admirers, including the writer, Leo Tolstoy. During their time in exile, the Dekabrists fundamentally influenced Siberian life. Their presence was felt absolutely culturally and economically; political activity was so far removed from the pulse of national life that it was negligible. While in Petrovsky Zavod, the Dekabrists taught each other foreign languages, arts and crafts, and musical instruments. They established "academies" consisting of libraries, schools, and symposia.

In their settlements, the Dekabrists were fierce advocates of education and founded many schools for natives, the first of which opened in Nerchinsk. Schools were also established for women. The Dekabrists made a major contribution in the field of agriculture, introducing previously unknown crops such as vegetables, tobacco, rye, buckwheat, and barley, and advanced agricultural methods such as greenhouse cultivation. Trained doctors among the political exiles promoted and organized medical aid. The homes of prominent exiles such as Prince Sergei Volkonsky and Prince Sergei Trubetskoi became social centres on their premises.

Everywhere in Siberia, the Dekabrists triggered an intellectual awakening: literary writings, propaganda, newspapers and books from European Russia began to circulate in the eastern provinces, the local population developed a capacity for critical political observation. The Dekabrists even had some influence within the Siberian administration; Dimitry Zavalishin played a crucial role in developing and advocating Russian politics in the Far East.

Although the Dekabrists lived in isolation, their scientific activities encompassed Siberia at large including its culture, economy, administration, population, geography, botany, and ecology. In 1856, when Alexander II ascended the throne, the Dekabrists were granted amnesty, and their rights, privileges, were restored. Their children were given rights, privileges, and even titles for their fathers (as princes) even if their fathers' titles were not restored. However, not everyone chose to return to the West. Some were financially inhibited, others had no family and many were frail from age. For many, Siberia had become their home.

The exile of the Dekabrists led to the permanent implantation of an intelligentsia in Siberia. For the first time, a cultural, intellectual, and political elite came to Siberian society as permanent residents; They integrated with the land and participated together with the natives in its development.

Evaluation

With the failure of the Dekabrists; Russia's autocracy would continue for almost a century, even if serfdom was to be officially abolished in 1861 and the parliaments of Russia and Finland were to be established in 1905. Finland had a parliament since Alexander I, but the number of electors was limited. The Russian constitution of 1905 was called "*The basic laws*" as the Dekabrists had called it. Although the Dekabrists were defeated, they brought about some changes in the regime. Their discontent forced Nicholas I to turn his attention inward to address the issues of the empire. He included many Dekabrists who had joined his forces in Senate Square and who ultimately did not support the revolt despite their participation in Dekabrist meetings of his government (such as Benkendorf, appointed to monitor human rights, Muraviev-Vilensky, and others). In 1826, Speransky was appointed by Nicholas I to head the second section of His Imperial Majesty's own Chancellery, a committee formed to codify Russian law.

Empire

Speransky's liberal ideas were subsequently examined and elaborated by Konstantin Kavelin and Boris Chicherin. Although revolt was a forbidden subject during Nicholas' reign, Alexander Herzen placed the profiles of executed Dekabrists on the cover of his radical journal Polar Star.

Alexander Pushkin[21] dedicated poems to his Dekabrist friends; Nikolai Nekrasov, whose father served alongside the Dekabrists in Ukraine, wrote a long poem about the Dekabrist wives; and Leo Tolstoy began to write a novel about the liberal movement, which would later develop into war and peace.

During the Soviet era, Yuri Shaporin produced an opera entitled Dekabristi, about the revolt, with the libretto written by Aleksey Nikolayevich Tolstoy. It premiered at the Bolshoi Theatre on 23 June 1953.

Alexander Sergeevich Pushkin is your first cousin four times removed's partner's third cousin twice removed's 1st husband.

---

[21] More info and pictures are available at: https://en.wikipedia.org/wiki/Alexander_Pushkin

For the Dekabrists, the rebellion led Nicholas to turn away from the modernization program initiated by Peter the Great and defend the doctrine of orthodoxy, autocracy, and nationalism. The Dekabrists were to some extent part of the tradition of a long line of palace revolutionaries who wanted to place their candidate on the throne, but since the Dekabrists also wanted to implement classical liberalism, their rebellion has been considered the beginning of a revolutionary movement. The uprising was the first open break between the government and reformist sections of the Russian nobility, which was then to expand.

HANS JOHANN OTTO VON ROSEN 1870 – 1945

The influence of the nobility in Livonia/Latvia is over.

The Livonia Governorate was a governorate of the Russian Empire from 1721 to 1918, when it was divided between Estonia and Latvia at the Treaty of Brest Litovsk.

The governorate was administered independently by the local German Baltic nobility through a feudal "Lantdag". Between 1629 and 1721, Livonia had belonged to Sweden. The governorate consisted of 9 districts: Riga, Wolmar, Wenden, Walk, Dorpat, Pernau, Fellin, Werro and Arensburg (Saaremaa). When the Great Northern War ended in 1721, Sweden was allowed to cede Livonia to Russia at the Treaty of Nystad.

Hans Johann Otto von Rosen is your first cousin twice removed's husband's first cousin once removed's wife's father.

The "Lantdagen" was the name of the people's representation in the Livonian Governorate.

The German nobles fought hard to retain their privileges and the use of the German language.

After the Russian February Revolution in 1917, the northern part of the Governorate of Livonia merged with the Estonian Governorate to form a new independent Governorate, Estonia. The Autonomous Governorate of Estonia issued the Estonian Declaration of Independence in 1918, one day before Estonia was occupied by German troops after World War I. The rest of Livonia formed Latvia. There had also been a revolution in Russia in 1905, but it was put down in 1907.

It was the beginning of the end of the centuries-old Baltic-German nobility's influence in the Baltic States with the formation of the Baltic independent republics.

Baron Hans Johann Otto von Rosen[22] is just one example of how influence could cease and with what tenacity the nobility defended their privileges for as long as possible.

A question I wrestle with for many years is whether Johannes Ludvig August Brüsewitz should be replaced by Hans Johann Otto von Rosen in the table above? Johannes was married to Marri Wirro, mother of Marie Helene Elisabeth Wirro. Marri was 9 years older than Johannes and maybe it was an arranged marriage. Only some help with DNA testing might be able to reveal the truth?

He was baptized 1870-12-01 as a Lutheran in the church in the castle of Gross-Roop (Lielstraupe).

---

[22] More info and pictures are available at: https://www.geni.com/people/Hans-Johann-Otto-von-Rosen/6000000018309107722

His godparents were:

- Baron Johann von Rosen (grandfather), who carried his grandson at the baptism
- Baron Ernst von Campenhausen von Orellen, Landrath
- Greve Carl von Sievers
- Countess von Sievers, née von Wulf
- Baronessan Alexandrine von Rosen, née von Kissel
- Baronessan Marie von Campenhausen, née von Smitten, District Administrator

He became the last landowner of Schloss Gross Roop.

Included in this book is a translation of the work of the Latvian historian Pārsla Pētersone, which was based on 19 pages of handwritten notes made by Baron Johann Otto Hans von Rosen in 1926. The original text was written in German. Pārsla Pētersone wrote her article in Latvian, which I have now translated into English. A lot can go wrong in such a translation chain, both in terms of words and context. Parts of the introductory text also come from the work of Pārsla Pētersone.

The article was based on a manuscript kept in the State Historical Archives of Latvia, a manuscript of personal memories written by Baron Johann Otto Hans von Rosen in 1926 in Lielstraupe (Gross Roop), in which he recounts his experiences in the Baltic States, Russia and Germany from the late 1800s to the mid-1920s.

His memories begin in the late 1800s in the family's beautiful castle Lielstraupe - an architectural and cultural monumental castle that was built as early as 1263 and burned down in 1905 by revolutionaries, and after that only the frame of the castle remained, which after significant repairs and reconstructions was rebuilt.

He also recalls his participation in Russia's First Council and gives his views on the causes and course of the First World War based on his own experiences.

The manuscript describes Hans von Rosen's feelings about the post-war political changes and the agrarian reform of the 1920s.

He lived in a very turbulent political time, where he lived through the revolution of 1905, the events of the First World War and the drastic political development after the war with the formation of the Republic of Latvia, a new generation of rulers that meant that Hans von Rosen had to give up his property and finally leave the country to end his days in Schwerin, Germany, where his wife originated from.

He belonged to an old noble family from Vidzeme, whose representatives had been awarded the title of baron already during the Holy Roman Empire in 1693, in later generations it was supplemented with the title of Swedish baron, Swedish count, French count and marquis. Russia also appointed; as a thank you for faithful service, members of the family of barons in 1855.

He lived according to what he himself describes a conscientious life, his most sacred task in life was to preserve and safeguard the family's honour and traditions in the Baltic German homeland.

He describes the major political events and gives his interpretation of them.

Already in the middle of the 14th century, Voldemārs von Rozens lived here, he also owned Mazstraupe, Stalbes, Auciems, Raiskums, Dikļi and Augstroze.

In the early 1600s, the Swedish government took the castle away from von Rosen's family in order to punish the family for being loyal to the

Polish king. Several centuries later, in 1857, the family regained its ancient property, and its last member, Baron Hans Johann Otto von Rosen, lived here until his departure for Germany in 1939. The fact that Sweden was able to deprive Baltic Germans of property in the Baltic States was due to the fact that Sweden had control over the Baltic States between 1560 and 1710, in a time that many have later called the good Swedish era, something that may not have been so good if you look at it a little more closely considering how taxation of the people was conducted. The notes also offer an opportunity to look at the events already known in Latvia's history with a little new eye, based on a personal observation on the spot that can provide a supplementary description of the events. Hans von Rosen was a cog in the "big politics" that took place in the Baltic States and which he generously shares with the reader with new facts and opinions.

Hans von Rosen (JOHvR) studied between 1882 and 1888 at the German high school (Gymnasium Kaiser Alexander II. zu Birkenruh at Wenden (Cēsis today); Bērzaine in Latvia).

The school[23] was closed down in 1892 when it was no longer allowed to teach in German, only in Russian.

In 1905, after the Russian Revolution, the school reopened and existed until 1915.

After high school, Hans von Rosen studied at the universities of Dorpat (Tartu), Berlin and Halle.

According to his matriculation book numbered 1943/81, Johann Frhr. (Baron) v. Rosen enrolled at the Faculty of Philosophy at the Friedrich-

---

[23] More info and pictures are available at: https://de.wikipedia.org/wiki/Landesgymnasium_Birkenruh

Wilhelm University in Berlin from 18.11.1890 to 22.05.1891 where he studied Cameralism [German: Cameralia or Kameralwissenschaft], a type of political and economic administration.

At the University of Halle, he wrote an essay on Socialism about the Russian philosopher Alexander Herzen, which he defended orally in an excellent way.

It also included a number of courses within the framework of his doctoral thesis, agricultural science, philosophy and economics.

Without knowing it, perhaps the essay on socialism included how to relate to the various aspects of agricultural science, philosophy and economics and what answers socialism could offer there as an alternative to the political system of the time?

JOHvR presented his work on Alexander Herzen to the Dean, Professor Dr. Conrad, at the Faculty of Philosophy at Königl. Friedrichs-Universität Halle-Wittenberg Halle, 8. June 1893.

Professor Conrad praises the work that JOHvR had done on Alexander Iwanowitsch Herzen.

It was not considered an easy task to collect and systematically organize the many individual pieces that JOHvR had succeeded with. The author had succeeded in creating a very clear, interesting and well-written account of socialism.

During his studies, he received a number of reprimands for various unaccepted acts during his studies in Germany. He had insulted a fellow student and another he had challenged to a duel according to a report I have. In summary, he left his doctoral studies without taking his doctorate with him, his diploma lacked a seal.

Social career Hans von Rosen

After completing his studies in 1893, Hans von Rosen returned to Livonia/Russia and settled on his estate, where he devoted himself to agriculture and became active in social and political activities in the community.

Notes by Hans von Rosen

Memoirs written by Baron Hans von Rosen, Lielstraupe, Latvia 1926

I was born on September 30, 1870, as the second oldest of 6 brothers (on October 12 according to the old calendar) at Lielstraupe Castle. My parents were Baron Friedrich Rosen and his wife Virginia (Ina), née Boltho von Hohenbach.

The eldest brother Conrad, who was 1 year older than me and was a very talented person, died of tuberculosis at the age of 18 in Falkenstein in the Taunus. The third brother, Woldemar, born in 1874, and later owner of Rosenbeck Manor, served in the Russian army and was killed in the 1915 war at Tauerkaln, Courland. My other 3 brothers died in infancy after only a few months.

In the Five Gateways genealogy, you can read the following about the von Rosen family:

Q2. Friedrich von Rosen, b. at Novgorod 16 Oct 1833, d. at Gross-Roop 7 Mar 1893, of Gross-Roop, Lieutenant in Russian service, m. at Mitau 11 Oct 1865 to Karoline Virginie Thekla Boltho von Hohenbach (b.1 Dec 1842, d. at Gross-Roop 17 June 1893), daughter of Guido Boltho von Hohenbach, of Alt-Wohlfahrt and Mitzhof in Courland (d. 1862) and his wife Luise von Lieven zu Dünhof.

- R1. Conrad Johann von Rosen, b. at Gross-Roop 19 May 1869, d. at Falkenstein in the Taunus 11/23 apr.1888.

64

- R2. Johann Otto von Rosen, may have had descendents (vilket denna bok visar)
- R3. Woldemar Friedrich Johann von Rosen, b. at Gross-Roop 5 Nov. 1874, killed in action at Tauerkaln in Courland 17 Aug. 1915, of Roperbeck and Maikendorf, in Russian service, m. at Tegasch 1 Jul. 1909 to Margaretha Elisabeth Constanze Eugenie von Samson Himmelstjerna zu Sepkull (b. at Kaugershof 16 May 1878).
- R4. another three sons, died young.

Under R2. Can you read that Johann Otto von Rosen, may have had descendents. Nothing about the actual relationships with 6 daughters that he had in his marriage to his wife. Why the information is so scarce about R2, becomes a bit of a mystery as the information about this branch of von Rosen describes events in 1915, when Johann Otto von Rosen was already married and had his 6 daughters with his wife. Could it allude to the expression "may have had descendents" and that something had come to light that made the author of "Five gateways genealogy" unable to record the correct information?

Lielstraupe slott 1928 (Negativ NVM-nr. 12 470)

My parents first gave me education at home, then I had a home teacher, Viktors Diederichs. In 1882 I entered the Bērzaine Gymnasium as a boarder (my parents moved to Cēsis) and in 1888 I graduated.

In the spring of 1889, to treat an ear injury, I travelled to Halle, Germany. I stayed there during 1889 - 1890 and studied economics and agriculture.

I continued my studies in 1890–1891 in Berlin, where I was particularly interested in Professor Treitschke's lectures on political issues. A year later, I moved to the University of Tartu and became a member of the Livonian Association, a membership that pleased me from the bottom of my heart all my life.

I finished my studies in Halle. In 1893 I received my doctorate in philosophy with the study "Die sozialpolitische Idéen" by Alexander Herzen (pseudonym Otto von Sperber, published by Duncker and Humboldt in Leipzig).

My father died in May 1893 and my mother died in June of the same year, both having heart attacks. When my father died, the responsibility for the property passed to my grandmother for the rest of her life, but in the spring of 1894, I took over responsibility for Lielstraupe.

I did not become a full owner of Lielstraupe until 1905, when my grandmother died. On August 15, 1898, I married Jenny von Vietinghofff-Scheel from Jungfernhof and we had a happy marriage until her untimely death in April 1915.

We had six daughters: Anna, Rita, Sofija, Benedikte, Jeanette and Lisette. Anna and Rita are married to two cousins from the von Hahn family, and Benedikte has just gotten engaged to Walter von Wahl from Pajus Manor.

During the Latvian (Russian) Revolution of 1905, the murderers burned down our old castle Lielstraupe, only the walls remained. But the building was rebuilt and, in the autumn of 1909, we were able to move in again. In the summers we live here now too, even though the fleeing Russians destroyed the sites during the First World War, especially after the fall of Riga in August 1917.

It is said that when the then Rosen family's owners; Hans von Rosen heard about other landowners' castles being turned to ashes by peasants, the family's possessions were evacuated to Riga and, after coordinating with the local rebels, the castle was burned down. The property was insured for a significant amount. But one should probably be careful when it comes to such rumours. After the war, Lielstraupe was used as an administrative centre for tractors by the Soviet local administration.

From 1963, Straupe was used for the rehabilitation of addicts, something that only ended in 2018. Discussions are underway on how to take advantage of the castle and restore it.

As with all castles, there are legends and this castle is no exception. In ancient times, the castles of Lielstraupe[24] and Mazstraupe were connected by an underground passage that ran under the river Brasla. In Lielstraupe it started in the cellar of the castle and continued up to the tower of Mazstraupe Castle. During the Polish rule in Lielstraupe there was a nunnery. In Mazstraupe, Polish hussars were stationed. Through the underground passage, the hussars often visited Lielstraupe Castle. In the garden of the castle, couples met and the glowing whispers were not devoted to Jesus Christ at all. As a testament to these love encounters, the carcasses of newborn babies can testify to that were later found when the castle's moat was cleared.

---

[24] More info and pictures are available at: https://en.wikipedia.org/wiki/Lielstraupe_Castle

Lielstraupe slott 1920

The picture shows a run-down castle after it was confiscated in 1920.

An interesting detail is that the castle has an integrated church in its building and is said to be the only castle in Latvia to have one.

When I took over the administration of Lielstraupe in 1894, there were 100 farms on its territory, after the sale of farms to the peasants, 70 remained, with a total area of 8,000 ha. After the confiscation of the properties under the Latvian agrarian reform (without compensation), only 50 hectares remain.

I started my career in 1894 as head of the parish in Straupe parish, where my main task was to oversee the roads within Straupe parish. After a few years, I left this position and became responsible for the church in Straupe. As a result of my leadership of the church and the school, based on the church's conventions and recommendations, a concern was created for the pastor in Straupe. At the same time, I was elected deputy for the Riga-Valmiera district by the Diet in 1899.

I joined the Livonian nobility convention and my social life consisted mainly of various tasks within the knighthood. At that time, Baron Friedrich Meyendorff, "Marshall of the Land", was the spokesperson for the knighthood and until his death I was involved in the introduction of the gentlemen's inspiring plans.

I led the deputy members of the county council while the parliament (parliament) met under the leadership of the then sitting baron of the court, the member of parliament Baron Tiesenhausen.

During the plenary sessions, the two chambers met, where they took the most important decisions between the various formal parliamentary sessions.

It was a strong period of Russification; the Russian language was to be introduced in all educational and state institutions.

In St. Petersburg, the political winds were dominated by bureaucratic self-government, in which the power of all institutions was concentrated in the hands of the Russian establishment at the expense of the local authorities. In the situation prevailing at the time, the knights tried as much as possible to promote the German education of the Baltic German youth in the church schools in St. Petersburg and by awarding scholarships for later studies in Germany. In addition to the struggle to preserve Germany in the first years of change, a debate arose at the Landowners' Convention as to whether it was necessary to continue to have overall responsibility within the administration for the construction of roads.

They had some success in the debate on both issues. The leading role of the knighthood in the management of road construction was recognized and a fund for road construction was created. The Baltic nobles, who were the only ones in the entire empire, were also compensated for their lost right to sell vodka. The fact that the Tsar made a decision in favour of the Baltic nobles in this matter can be attributed to Marshal Baron Meyendorff and Saaremaa Marshal von Ekesparre. They managed to get the support of Grand Duke Mikhail, the president of the Senate, who himself raised the issue with the tsar.

70

In addition to working for the Knights' Convention, I held a position as a county representative.

I was also responsible for the construction of roads, railways and bridges in the district of Riga (and for a short time also Cēsis). The settlers' commission also had to be monitored, which is why I always spent two weeks in Riga during the mobilization - in October. As well as a number of other mixed assignments.

The conflicts with government agencies began when I was chairman of the tax commission. It was an extensive contribution from the Knights of Vidzeme to the legislative field, but I strongly criticized it in the Diet of 1896. In addition, I am very active in the credit committee (Vidzeme Manor Credit Association) and as the director of the Vidzeme River Regulatory Association.

The Gauja-Daugava Canal was built with the help of private donations for the members of the organization, the works were supervised by Count Berg-Sagnitz, the owner of the Sangaste estate. The conversations and meetings related to the project were interesting and educational, and because of the canal construction, I had the opportunity to travel to Berlin to sign a contract.

For a short time, I was entrusted with the administration of the Bērzaine estate, but due to the Russification pressure of the high school operating there, the school was closed in 1892 following a decision of the Diet.

An important area of knighthood was the concern for the development of health care, as evidenced by the construction of a medical facility in rural Strenči, and where I gave a short speech in Latvian at the inauguration ceremony.

As a member of the Vidzeme Imperial General and Economic Society (Kaiserliche Livländische Gemeinnützige und Öconomische Societät), I was able to use my knowledge in the economic field. The meetings, partly open, partly closed, took place every year in January in Tartu.

In the summer, trips to mansions were organized together with business experts.

Hans von Rosen at the Knights' Convention 1908

One of the more vivid memories that has lingered with me was a summer meeting with Baron Stael at Neu Anzen Manor and with Erika von Oetingen at Pölks Manor. The first showed the manor's trout pond, the second - different meadow cultures. Together with the Vidzeme Foresters' Association, I also participated in an excursion to the forests of the Euseküll Manor in Viljandi County.

Shortly after the Japanese War started in 1904, there was a sharp turn in the political life of Russia and, consequently, Vidzeme. The defeats and incentives of secret revolutionary organizations forced the government to decide to involve local authorities and the people in the public administration. In order for this to happen, the most ingenious Russian statesman of his time, Prime Minister

Vitte, decided to set up committees, which simply began to be called public com-
mittees (comites der salus publica). They brought together representatives of
the government and all walks of life, and under the leadership of the governor,
various current issues were discussed, mostly of an economic nature, but they
also touched on political topics. There was talk of tax equalization and road
construction obligations in rural areas, as well as the limitation of the privileges
of chivalry. I had to speak in Russian for the first time at one of these committee
meetings.

The stone was rolling: the meeting of 1905 already brought together the most
prominent members of the council of the province - representatives of knights,
burghers and peasants, with whom I also discussed the reform project. Deci-
sions in the spirit of the times were also taken by the Diet in the summer of
1905, especially the drafting of the province's new constitution, in the process
it was decided to involve representatives of agriculture. According to the draft,
the Diet (Parliament) would leave a number of issues to the new authorities,
leaving out only problems directly related to the knighthood and its competence.

I represented the interests of those who were non-wealthy members of society
in Parliament, and when this competence was transferred to the newly created
provincial authorities, I had to leave, but the Treasury of Parliament still paid
me for all my living expenses.

A revolutionary movement began to grow in society, which took the form of
the killing of owners of mansions, pastors and officials, recurrent social disturb-
ances, the organization of demonstrations against the tsar, etc.

In rural areas, under the leadership of socialist parties, anti-state and anti-
church ideas are spread through proclamations and gatherings. At that time,
we established a self-defence force and regularly guarded the church in Straupe.
In the summer of 1905, the storm had not yet reached here, but one Sunday,

when the news of an armed attack during the funeral came from Vidriži, I asked for and received troops for protection.

The revolutionary movement also spread within the postal and railway systems.

The Tsar tried to respond by convening Parliament for consultative purposes. A manifesto was issued on October 17, 1905, laying the groundwork for a constitution establishing legislation and proclaiming freedom of religion, speech, and assembly.

I was in Riga at the time where I participated in the recruitment of recruits. There was a lack of discipline so I could only complete the task with great effort.

In the autumn, the situation became calmer, but at the end of November it flared up again. In line with the political goal of reducing the influence of landowners in rural areas, the men's homes were hit the most. While my family and I were living in Riga during the Knights' Convention, a gang of robbers led by a farmer from Nītaure also set fire to Lielstraupe Castle.

A few days earlier, under the leadership of the members of the Social-Democratic Federal Committee, I went to Lielvārde to obtain the release of a German gentleman and imprisoned ladies who had been arrested by the revolutionary masses. For this I had to pay 500 roubles, as well as publicly apologize to the assembled masses.

Because of the arrests, the public asked for the support of the Russian dragoons, but these were attacked and driven away by the armed masses. In the countryside the power of the government was completely paralyzed, the railways were in the hands of the revolutionaries.

Lieslstraupe Castle 1905 burnt down

In Riga, where the owners of the southern Livonian mansions and pastors and their families fled, order was maintained only because of fear of the German self-defence forces. At the last moment, sentry troops arrived from St. Petersburg and began punitive expeditions and restored order.

In the spring of 1906, together with the family I had sent to Berlin for the winter, we moved back to Straupe. We settled in a villa built in 1898, which was located on a plot of land purchased by the owner of the Mazstraupe Riebiņi pub, and I began, with the help of the architect Bockslaff, to restore the castle.

At the same time, I also participated in the implementation of new tasks for the Knights of Vidzemes, called for by the new times. An opportunity to rebuild German schools must be found.

After interesting work within the Commission and a long debate in the Parliament, it was decided to reopen the classical high school with a boarding school in Bērzaine. At the inauguration ceremony I spoke to those present - in the same room where I experienced the first opening of the school in 1882, where in 1892

I said goodbye on behalf of former pupils, where in the autumn of 1914 the school was to be used as a military hospital.

The reopening of the school in August 1906 was overshadowed by the news of the murder of the pastor of Lielvārde, Zimmermann and his wife, the day before. For another month, peaceful life in the countryside was disrupted by murderers. I found it particularly painful when my neighbour – the owner of Stalbe Manor, Campenhausen – was killed in the summer of 1906. Formally, the revolution was suppressed, but protests continued in the countryside and real peace did not arrive until 1907. At that time, order was maintained throughout the country, and under the leadership of the Interior Minister Stolipin, the government began to make decisive decisions. The reforms initiated by the knighthood continued.

In 1906, a council was convened under the chairmanship of the Baltic Governor-General.

This institution, in which I also participated, was set up on the initiative of the knighthood.

Representatives from all three Baltic provinces jointly drafted laws to reform the administrative system, the church, schools, courts, and agricultural legislation and submitted them to the government for approval, but the proposals were not approved there. Legislation engaged in new tasks, the most important of which were parliamentary institutions - the State Duma and the State Council.

In 1906, only Latvian and Estonian representatives from the Baltic provinces were elected to the State Duma, which had been established as a result of the first purely democratic vote.

When the Second Duma, after its dissolution, was also unable to work due to radicalism, on June 3, 1907, a manifesto was issued restricting the right to vote,

which became much more conservative. The Coup of June 1907, sometimes referred to as the Coup of Stolipin, is the name commonly referred to as the dissolution of the Second Duma of the Russian Empire, the arrest of certain members, and a fundamental change in the Russian electoral law by Tsar Nicholas
II.

Nicholas II's inaugural address to the Duma in 1906

Through indirect elections, separate representations were established for
large and small landowners, parishes as well as burghers, and now even a small
but culturally important German minority could enter parliament.

In the autumn of 1907, I, together with the following gentlemen, was elected
to the Diet as a representative of the large landowners in Vidzeme:

-   Baron Alexander Meyendorff, owner of Mazstraupe – representing the
    entire province.
-   Brakmann, the mayor of Pärnu as a representative of the citizens.

- Lawyer Ervins Morits - representing Riga. When Moritz died, he was replaced by Robert Eckhardt.
- Baron Hamilkar Fölkersahm from Courland as a representative of the country's major landowners.
- Baron Alfred Schilling of Estonia.
- Baron Otto Beneke, represented the Estonian city of Reval.

All these gentlemen have been good colleagues of mine for five years.

At first, I only had a temporary mandate for one year, because the idea was that Baron Pilar would take the place, but he was elected Land Marschall in 1908.

It changed everything and I had to keep my job longer. In 1908 I was elected county representative, but already in 1909, I resigned because my duties could not be combined with the mandate as a member of the Council of State Duma.

In the autumn of 1911, I was elected to the County Council, but in an internal conflict in the late autumn of 1912, I resigned most of the assignments together with five other councillors and members of parliament.

In May 1914, I was re-elected to the Diet, a position I held until June 1920, when the Latvian Parliament abolished the knightly institutions.

Hans von Rosen 1908

From the autumn of 1919 until the end, I also served as deputy Land Marschall, as the last Land Marschall, Stryk, elected in 1918, resigned in January 1919.

From 1907 to 1912 I was a member of the Third State Duma. From the second winter I lived with my family in Tsarskoye Selo, very close to the Tsar's palace. During the first winter, the Tsar and the Tsarina invited us right-wing MPs and representatives of the Centre parties to a luxurious reception in the great palace.

The evening was opened by the Tsar himself with a short and meaningful speech. The tsarina, who led the little heir to the throne by the hand, left a truly majestic impression: her wonderful features on her face radiated a deep seriousness. I got the same impression when I saw him in 1913 at the celebration of the 300th anniversary of the Romanov family in the Knights' Hall in the Winter Palace. When the heir to the throne was unable to parade due to his illness (he suffered from haemophilia), he was carried by a strong Cossack. Unlike the young Tsarina Aleksandra, the old Tsarina - her mother - came to the festivities with hard, loud steps and bright make-up and with dyed hair.

Together with other Baltic MPs, I joined the October 17 faction, a national liberal party that originally consisted of a strong core of 150 men, with the right and moderate right (later nationalists) on one side and the peaceful restorers, the constitutional democrats (cadets), the workers' group and the Social Democrats on the other side. Initially, the Octobrists agreed with the right on most issues, and together they supported the government. At the beginning of the Third City Council, Prime Minister Stolipin was also able to come up with advice and gain support in the drafting of agricultural laws with the aim of creating private farmers.

*The leader of the Octobrists was Alexander Guchkov, a Moscow businessman by origin, an unusually energetic and clever, at the same time closed-minded, intelligent and adventurous man who appeared not only to be energetic but also to sincere. However, his seclusion left a negative impression. Deep down, he was a Democrat and a Republican, but also a fanatical nationalist. He respected us Baltic Germans and treated us very well. He showed a negative attitude towards the Russification policy of the anti-Finnish way, especially in the attempts to call for war in the newspaper **Новое время (New Times)** with his influence.*

An important figure among the Baltic deputies was Baron Alexander Eeien-
dorf, who was elected second vice-president of the Council.

The first president at that time was Homyakov (Хомяков), an old Russian
representative of the noble families, first vice president - Volkonsky
(Волконский).

Meyendorff, with his extensive knowledge and opinions, always received at-
tention in his surroundings, he always stood up for the defender, he showed
special compassion for Finland's issue. His sacrifice for others knew no bounds
to protect the Germans during the war.

Since I was the owner of Mazstraupe's neighbouring farm - Lielstraupe - we
became friends. I very much appreciate the opportunity to work with this great
personality, even if our political views did not always coincide. He was a Rus-
sian-oriented cosmopolitan, but Germans and the German were always my fo-
cus of political attention.

The Manifesto of October 17, 1905, proclaimed religious freedom in Russia.
This created a need for new laws, first and foremost regarding free elections.
The alternates in the Council who worked on this issue were brought together
in a separate commission where I was elected its deputy head and was therefore
actively involved in the work.

I made a long speech on this question in the Duma for the first time, and I
also made a few shorter speeches later, as in the response to the socialist Gegec-
chori's demands on the Baltic nobility and the Social Democrats' interpretation
of the punitive expeditions of 1905.

In general, there has been an increasing effort to restrict democratic legisla-
tion.

Over time, more and more reactionary tendencies arose in which the govern-
ment, led by Stolipin, slid more and more towards the national orientation and

gained the support of the majority of the October party, so Pan-Slavism prevailed. First, they took care of Finland, then a conflict arose with Poland over the area of Cholm (Chelm). Chelm is located in eastern Poland near the border with Ukraine. Then an anti-German campaign was launched against the German colonists' estates in Pievolga (Volga area).

The revolutionary Russian movement that with the averted revolution of 1905 affected the various provinces of the Russian Empire. Karl Stumpp describes well in his book: "Die Russlands-Deutschen" life in the various provinces of the Russian Empire.

The annexation of Bosnia and Herzegovina in 1908 encouraged active propaganda in the districts of Reni and Volyn and was discussed in the Council of State. In the light of these events, talks about war with Germany soon became more and more clear. In this situation, the government took a number of steps to equip its troops and navy. In order to get a hearing on borrowing for the navy's armament, the Minister for Maritime Affairs took us MEPs twice on his boat to Kronstadt, where he was very well received.

The officer who accompanied us at Kronstadt and described the details of the visit concluded by expressing his desire to shoot Germany down - which frightened me.

At the same time, cooperation with the French and English became increasingly close, this was especially the case during visits to parliamentarians in Paris and London in 1911 and 1912. In general, no military feeling was expressed during the winter visit of French deputies and senators in 1911, as was the case in early 1912 when the British were visited. At the banquet, a general stressed that the planned military cooperation would be welcome in all respects, and in response to a question from one of those present, he replied with the words немцев бить (defeat the Germans).

We Baltic Germans did not show any concern at first.

The political mood was also influenced by the Tsar's visit to Riga in 1910 on the occasion of the 200th anniversary of the annexation of Vidzeme to Russia. The solemn speeches in the House of Nobility were praised, in which I also participated, and my heartfelt congratulations were given. I had a long conversation with Stolipin on that occasion, during which he invited me to his home in St. Petersburg.

Of course, the Baltic issue was not given much attention on this occasion.

At the beginning of the new wave of legislation in 1912, the Baltic church administrations, county administrations, etc., were expected to address important issues in order to avoid conflicts and unrest in society.

Since I didn't know enough Russian at the time and my hearing was deteriorating, I didn't feel confident that I would be able to do my job well, so I explained to chivalry that I didn't want to be re-elected after my five-year term. In the spring of 1912, I left the council. In the autumn of the same year, Baron Nikolai Wolff was elected as my successor.

Instead, I was unexpectedly elected to the Council of State as the successor to Baron Heinrich Tiesenhausen.

The nomination of me as a minister, which took place in the House of Nobility in Riga in October 1912, as a representative of the large landowners of Vidzeme, was facilitated by the conflict between Baron Pilar, the Land Marschall and the convent of the nobility, which began in 1908.

After a vote, Baron Pilar was elected as a minister as a representative of the entire nobility, which was also in our interest. The root cause of the disagreement probably lay in Pilar's knowledgeable, independent, and hypersensitive nature, which made him a leader in political struggles, but in peaceful political work he found it difficult to respect the Diet and the directives and decisions of the Convention, especially if he did not agree. The personality of the former Land Marshal Friedrich Meyendorff could serve as an example of such an official, he acted in complete agreement with the representatives of the knights. When church issues were discussed, the difference of opinion was marked.

After the experience of the revolution of 1905, a new group was formed within the knighthood - the Old Liberals/Altliberals, to which Pilar, as well as the County Councillors' Tiesenhausen, Strandmann, Stackelberg, Gersdorff, Wilhelm Stael, Kurt Anrep and also Friedrich Meyendorff (he fell ill shortly after he left his post and died in the spring of 1911), joined, but we believed that in the everyday work with Latvians and Estonians we could maintain peaceful relations.

We, the Young Conservatives, believed that, in order to maintain peace, in a situation where progress was being made in the religious field, we could allow a division into German and non-German churches. Since the Diet did not approve this, we proposed that the tax on land should be abolished, which would reduce the German minority from overly burdensome taxes.

The distribution was also predictable, the need to maintain the church through taxes would only promote it.

The ideas opposed by the entire spiritual and secular world at the time, with the exception of Pastor Keller and Lawyer Schoeler, later formed the basis of Latvia's new religious life.

Unlike Land Marschall Pilar's group of Old Liberals, the number of German nationalists (some seen as advocates of German accession) increased in our group, with its spiritual leaders Siwers, Eric Oettinger, and Max Anrep.

On the contrary, Pilar took a Russian-oriented stance. In most cases, the dividing line between the two groups was not strictly defined. As for the German national question, Friedrich Meyendorff and Strandmann always accepted our *views, they also participated in the formation of the German Association and German schools, while the pro-Russian Ferdi Liphart and Eduard Nolcken even protested against Pilar on the question of independence and liberalization of the rights of the country's citizens, but in the normalization of the German-Russian antagonism; In contrast to our energetic army comrades, they showed complete helplessness.*

In general, the contradictions on the national question were mainly due to a lack of understanding. The conflict was well illustrated by the election of a minister at the Knights' Convention in December 1912. Pilar was clearly accused of nominating himself, evading me and of delegating an Estonian to the mandate of the Russian nobility, with the result that the people of Livonia lost one vote. Due to the escalating controversy, Pilar later had to announce his resignation.

Since he realized that he did not have the support of the majority in the Convention, he wanted to submit the decision to the Parliament. In response, six County Councillors (Maxis Sievers, Arveds Etingens (Oettingen), Erik Ettingens, Arveds Strandmann, Harri Stryk and I) and all ordinary members present (three absent) resigned. When the new Land Marschall was elected to the Diet a few days later, we did not participate, and other people took part in the election.

Our self-esteem led us to do so, because Pilar had said that he did not find it possible to cooperate with the majority of the Convention. It was only when he withdrew his declaration for his re-election in 1914 that we had the opportunity to return to the Convention: almost all the County Councillors who had been elected to our seats resigned loyally, thus paving the way for us - in 1914 Strandman, Arved Oettingen and I were re-elected. This episode shook us.

The conflict also had a negative impact in our camp and created moral con-
fusion. The Land Marschall, as well as members of the Convention's opposition,
acted in good faith. He proved to be a real tactician and diplomat, better suited
to find psychological solutions in the deliberations of the Diet.

Chivalry has always tried to unite in a particular group; the group tolerates
the independence of a leader better than the supremacy of a congress. In addi-
tion, the contradictions were complex and difficult to understand.

When WWI started shortly after our return, the conflict lost all its power
and foundation.

Echoes of what happened were felt at the 1918 elections to Land Marschall,
when Pilar did not get a majority. This was due to his cool attitude towards
German ideas. He himself mentioned in his memoirs that the desired policy of
reconciliation of peoples did not generate support from the majority.

But Pilar's merits for the sake of the country will undoubtedly remain, and
in the summer of 1925, I was able to make a commendatory speech at his coffin
with complete conviction.

The work of the Government was made interesting by contacts with promi-
nent personalities. All the former ministers gathered there, like the well-known
Vite, who, like a roaring lion, completely isolated from the coalition, openly
sought power again. We Balts belonged to the Centre Party. In addition to Pilar,
I was also represented by Baron Schilling, the Estonian representative, Count
Pahlen of Courland and the former Marshal of Saaremaa von Ekesparre, ap-
pointed by His Majesty as a member of the Council of State.

As in the municipal council, I focused mainly on the field of information:
from 1907 to 1914 I regularly sent reports to all the conventions and parlia-
ments concerning the activities of the City Council and the State Council,
which should now be in the collection of knightly documents in the State

Archives of Latvia. In the autumn of 1912, a summary report on the past five-year plan was published by the State Duma.

I appeared only once in the Council of State - on the question of the planned prohibition of parishes, which was intended to restrict spiritual activities in mansions. I, Mrs Pilar and Mr Schilling spoke against the proposal and its implementation was prevented. Public speaking was not a problem for me, it brought me joy, but it always required careful preparation, and if success was expected from the speech, I memorized whole sentences. I was not equipped with the ability to skilfully oppose or respond to a discussion. I often had to speak in the Diets. The first time in 1896 on the question of the land tax reform, which I opposed at the time, as well as a meeting on the admission of new people to the aristocracy, in which I represented an exclusive opinion.

Of all the speeches in the Diet, my speech in 1902 on the founding of a business school in Wiland and my work from 1910 on churches received the greatest estimates. In both cases, it had practical consequences. I was particularly pleased to speak to the Baltic youth. Good occasions to speak were at the centenary celebrations of Livonia in 1922, at the Livonian Convention in Riga in 1926 and on a few other occasions. We were also lucky enough to give a speech to our guests from the centenary celebration of Rigensis.

For three years, from 1912 to 1915, I was a member of the Council of State. To be with the family, over the winter of 1913/1914 we rented an apartment in a suburb of Lesnaya. The 300th anniversary of the Romanov dynasty also fell during this time of extremely bright but strict celebrations. In his impersonally restrained way, the Tsar paralyzed those present with his silent wife and retinue of the small heirs to the throne.

After being elected a minister, I had to appear before the Tsar at the Winter Palace. It was a small reception for eight people.

We were asked to address the Tsar himself, because he was unable to start a conversation. The impression I got of him during the short minutes of the conversation strengthened my previous opinion. He was insecure, suspicious, without willpower and interest in other people, I could feel that trust was replaced by ambition. The tragic end of his life and the way he endured it leads us to soften our condemnation today.

During my stay in St. Petersburg, I participated every year as a representative of the nobility of Livonia in meetings with Russian nobles, and because of a short speech I made once, I was also elected to the University Committee. This institution had little political significance, there were not enough competent people, moreover, there were all kinds of intrigues and gossip, fruitful discussions were not appreciated. We Balts were highly respected in these circles.

I participated in the meetings of the Council of the Nobles until 1916. At the end of the 1915 parliamentary term, I left the Government. After my wife's death in the spring of 1915, I had to abstain at least partially from public life and devote more attention to my family. That's why I refused to stand for election. My successor was Eduard Nolcken.

At the beginning of the war, the atmosphere in St. Petersburg was very unpleasant.

However, our colleagues in the Government protected us badly. Their polite behaviour was in sharp contrast to the delegates of the Octobrists, who slandered the Baltic States and betrayed the party. Everywhere - in the streets and in gatherings - there was a fanatical hatred of the Germans, and participation in patriotic demonstrations that could not be avoided was intolerable. That is why I was happy to leave my position as a minister.

We Balts foresaw the outbreak of war with Germany in advance. Whenever possible, I tried to warn the native Germans of the dangers ahead, especially the

88

well-known German naval officer Keyserling and the military attaché von Eggeling. It was only then that I realized when I complained that the embassy's diplomats and the Ministry of Foreign Affairs did not want to listen to such speech. The Balts were seen as undesirable elements that disturbed peace.

A few weeks before the war started, I talked to Embassy Counsellor von Leune about the possibility of war. The news I conveyed about individuals - for example, about the roles of Aleksandrs Petrovičs Izvoļskis (1856–1919) and Stolypin's cousin Neidhardt in the development of the nationalist orientation of the Council of State - was completely new.

Ambassador Count Pourtale, whom I met at a luncheon with my colleague Schilling in the spring of 1914, naively asked me how such unfriendly tones could be heard in Russia's loyal attitude to Germany, when Germany had supported Russia in the war against Turkey so much and no thanks for it.

Has the Tsar's visit to Berlin a year ago been forgotten?

In addition, the army and navy grew manifold during this time. The government's order provided for an annual increase in the number of recruits by 135,000. In Reval (Tallinn), the construction of a war port was quickly started. The second should be set up in Memel (Klaipeda), announced a senior representative of the Navy at the Council meeting. The tone was set by the newspaper Новое время (New Times), which fuelled the war tanks. One of the shareholders, Al. Falz-Fain, told me that in May 1914 there was a debate about the paper's foreign policy position, in contrast to Menshikov, Guchkov expressed clearly: clap your hands the war with the Germans can only help us: France takes Alsace-Lorraine, England - German colonies, we - Galicia, and then we banish Tsar Nicholas II.

With regard to the planned time of the outbreak of war, Minister Sazonova's statement in the Government's Committee on Foreign Affairs was significant. Loving the peace of the German Emperor allowed us to choose a suitable time.

In the summer of 1918, I was able to share this statement with an officer of the German General Staff, who, with my consent, published it in the newspaper *Norddeutsche Allgemeine Zeitung*. Kaiser Wilhelm also mentioned Sazonov's statement in a letter sent to Hindenburg in the Netherlands.

I was also told that Sazonov, when he took office, had received an explanation from the military regarding the state war industry: before 1914 we must not fight, from 1914 we can fight, in 1917 we must fight. It seems that some members of the Entente, especially England, wanted to postpone the start of the war for a couple of years - until the Russian army was tested.

But the military advocates, led by the Serbian king Grand Duke Nicholas and Grand Duke Peter Nikolayevich, as well as the wise but unserious war minister Sukhomlinov.

The War Minister's hesitation before the war was fortunate for Germany, but they decided to push the matter through earlier. If the war had begun later, the great superiority of the Russian army would undoubtedly have crushed the German army.

Immediately after the declaration of war, we met at a meeting of the Council of State. There was no limit to bourgeois patriotism and predictions of victory: German submission was planned within a few months, and prominent officers were ordered to obtain Berlin maps as soon as possible. On behalf of the Balkan Germans, Foelkersahm and Pilar declared their loyalty to the Council of State. Pilar said: "In the first days of the war, our Baltic country may become a battlefield, so we declare that the thoughts and feelings of all of us are focused on the unfortunate of this country and their crowned leader".

The public was given false reports of victories. The Battle of Tannenberg was described as an insignificant success for the German army, due to the numerical advantage, as well as on the well-developed railway network for organizing army transport. In St. Petersburg, confiscated German and Allied flags were displayed to the public in an exhibition. I went to see it and the first thing I saw was the flag of the German Singers' Association with the inscription - In Freund und Leid zum Lande sind wir stets bereit. Among the trophies was also the menu from the restaurant at the station in Lviv (Lemberg).

A few months later, warnings were already being heard that East Prussia's loss was irreversible. The grief of loss was soon followed by a deep depression. There was talk of the Russian army's weak support, lack of ammunition and clothing, for which Sukhomlinov was blamed, something he initially responded to with strange jokes, but where he was later forced to resign due to opposition pressure led by Gučkov. His successor in the War Ministry, Polivanov, a member of the Council of State and general to the Tsar, in whom he had high hopes, later after the revolution along with many other high-ranking generals, went over to the Bolsheviks.

Even later, the public tried to keep their spirits up with news of victories. The best seems to have been the fantastic announcement of the repulsion of the landing near Pärnu and the sinking of five German ships.

In fact, a German ship was sunk to save the port of Pärnu. The idea of blowing up and fleeing the big houses in Pärnu belonged to the commander of Pärnu, Rodzyanko.

They systematically looked for German atrocities to use as war propaganda. We, the members of the Government, regularly received brochures with the following information. I remember a story about Russian soldiers who were allegedly burned alive by the Germans. As proof, a picture was published with

91

Cossacks who had seen what had happened with their own eyes. Lying propaganda was also directed at Russian-German citizens, especially Balts, who were having a difficult time.

The Livonian German organization (Deutsche Verein) was closed shortly after the war broke out. The shutdown meeting of the organization in the Riga Dome Museum chaired by President Max Anrep and his deputy, Professor Kupffer, has remained indelible in my memory.

Suspicion and persecution of Baltic Germans soon began: for no reason, one by one were sent to Siberia, including my best friend and neighbour, a crusader of the Livonia Corporation - Baltazar von Campenhausen from Ungurmuiza.

22.VII.13. Sross Roop.

Lielstraupe Castle 1913

It was only thanks to the efforts of Alexander Meyendorff that he and his wife were not deported to Siberia, but were allowed to settle in Irkutsk. This happened despite the fact that the Balts had to fight their brothers in the war. In August 1915, my only brother Voldemar, owner of the Roperbeķi manor, who had married Els von Saxony six years ago, was killed near Tauerkaln in Courland.

At the beginning of the war, he was appointed reserve officer of the Second Pskov Dragoon Regiment, which took part in the fighting in East Prussia and Poland. Even though my brother had very poor hearing, he was not fired. He was killed in the forest in Tauerkaln. The body was taken to Straupe, where he was also buried. Soon after, a military investigation commission arrived from Cēsis' headquarters in Straupe to check that there was no ammunition in the chest, which was forbidden. Thanks to our faithful servant and his vigorous protest, because I was not there with my family at that time, the Kalmyks had to leave, they had achieved nothing.

I myself had the opportunity to expose a very serious accusation. Constantine von Rautenfeld, a seventy-year-old man known as a man of honour, was insulted by an unreasonable woman who claimed to have received money from a German plane. He was immediately arrested and imprisoned. The perpetrator was summoned for questioning, first at the headquarters in Cēsis, then at the headquarters in Pskov, where I accompanied him. It was only with great effort that I managed to get von Rautenfeld released, who needed innumerable guarantees from well-known people, until, in confrontation with the accused, he confessed that he had never seen him in his entire life.

The persecution of the Baltic Germans became more active with each passing month. German newspapers were banned, as was correspondence in German, and Germans were not allowed on the streets, railways, or other public places.

In the summer of 1915, the German army conquered Courland. Riga was threatened, so the Land Council moved its seat to Tartu, where congress meetings were also held.

Dissatisfaction with the Russian government and regime, especially in parliamentary circles, was growing more and more, especially against the tsar, who had become completely dependent on the predator Rasputin and his orders were unconditionally accompanied by all senior government officials.

Rasputin had had a noble upbringing and there was a certain similarity between him and Jesus when it came to his hair and beard and he had a look that drilled into you like a predator's. He may also have had the ability to hypnosis. The unfortunate Tsarina saw him as a God-given saint and trusted him blindly, especially after he managed to stop the bleeding in the heir to the throne, possibly by hypnosis. Rasputin was a strong opponent of the war with Germany and predicted in his prophecies the damage it would inflict on Russia.

I can say that the fortune seeker also acted in secret from the Tsarina. In the winter of 1916/1917, he was killed by a member of the Russian patriot group, Prince Yushovov and Puriškevich.

The fate of the dynasty was coming to an end and it had also lost its influence in conservative circles.

The revolution at the end of February 1917 and the overthrow of the Tsar continued without difficulty.

The process was facilitated by pressure from the Entente, which supported the German attitude towards the Tsar and Tsarina. The whole nation rejoiced at the overthrow of the Tsar.

The majority initially hoped for a constitutional monarchy with Parliament. Since the tsar denied the throne to his son, while his brother Mikhail wanted to accept the throne only with the consent of the popular assembly, the monarchy ceased to exist as there was no support for it.

Soon, the group of Gučkov and Milukov lost their grip on the development of the revolution, which shattered their original hopes of retaining the leadership of the republic. The former Socialist MP Kerensky, who had already been appointed Minister of Justice, was to be appointed very soon.

This hysterical doctrine of the obsessive Kerensky, who used his illusions of freedom to destroy old institutions and institutions and paved the way for the Bolsheviks, who achieved the final victory of the revolution of October 1917.

The overthrow of the monarchy granted a general amnesty to the Baltic Germans deported to Siberia and considered the possibility of returning to their homeland. After the overthrow of the tsar, who was the one to whom we had sworn allegiance, we felt no moral aversion to Russia, we only waited for the day when German troops would liberate us, all the more so when the influence of the Bolsheviks in the country increased and they took over the organizations.

Almost all of them with German-Baltic sympathies belonged to Germany from the beginning, only a few, whom the others called sick, stood on the Russian side behind a misunderstood loyalty. For a long time, some had quietly nurtured the idea of finally joining Germany. I also belong to this Baltic group. At the centre of the group was the owner of Skriveri manor Max Sievers.

After the First Russian Revolution in 1905, a Baltic Relief Society was founded in Berlin in 1908 under the leadership of Theodor Schiemann. Its members were mostly Reich Germans and the organization mainly served a narrow propaganda purpose to spread German interests among the Baltic Germans. As a result, contacts were established, providing opportunities for the rest of us to exchange ideas, but any further efforts were deemed forbidden. But with the outbreak of war, the dream became more real. At that time, especially after the German army crossed the Russian border and occupied Jelgava in the summer of 1915, there were only a few pessimists among us who did not believe in the realization of the idea, which is why we called them the goats of sorrow.

August 19, 1917 also struck the hour of the liberation of Riga, on August 17 I experienced the first bombing of the German army and saw the Russians fleeing. When I received a message that the Germans were crossing the Daugava

River near Ikšķile, I hurried to the family in Straupe, where we had to witness the retreat of completely humiliated Russian troops, who in a few hours, partly removed, partly completely destroyed, the manor's movable equipment - cattle, horses, household items, clothes.

When the situation became life-threatening, hoping to soon see the German rescuers, we made our way to the nearby forest. Unfortunately, expectations were not met, the Germans held their line about 20 miles from Straupe and only occupied this part of the country at the end of February 1918.

The interior of the castle was completely destroyed - we had to move to Cēsis, where acquaintances provided us with clothes and linen, because we had had everything confiscated.

In November, I went to Tartu to treat my eye disease, which threatened to lead to blindness. It was later in Riga that I was rescued by the wonderful man and doctor Baron Heinrich Krüdener.

At Christmas I wanted to return to Cēsis, but I had been told that the revolutionary committee was looking for me there. In the meantime, contact was established with Germany with the help of acquaintances in Stockholm, especially with the county representative Heinrich von Stryk from the manor in Voltveti (Tignitz) in Estonia. We learned from a Reich courier in August that Pilar and Dellingshausen had issued a statement that a request for occupation of the territory would be sent to the German General Staff on behalf of the people of Vidzeme and Estonia, thus providing the necessary political justification for the event.

In late autumn, a similar decision was made at the Knights' Convention, and the event, which was secretly carried out by the Land Marschallen, the Land Council and the Knights-Secretary of the Realm, received formal consent.

When we learned that Count Mirbach, former counsellor at the Embassy in St. Petersburg and former representative for maritime affairs, had come for talks with the Bolshevik government, which was conducting peace negotiations in Brest-Litovsk, I went to St. Petersburg to establish contact with Keyserling, whom I knew very well from before.

With the help of the Swedish ambassador, General Brändström, and the Swedish Consul, Hall, I had several meetings with Keyserling at the consulate's headquarters, where other Balts also participated. Keyserling used the meeting to find out the public's attitude to the German occupation through us.

Our young gentlemen, mainly students from Tartu, collected the necessary information from all over the province and sent it to us in St. Petersburg. Similarly, information was sent to Germany about Russian troops, which were in full collapse and had become a threat to the local population.

I still remember the sight of the Cossacks leaving their fallen comrades in a wonderfully cultivated, unharvested oat field near Cēsis.

In the outermost regions, which had not been plagued by the revolution, the Latvian and Estonian rural populations looked more and more forward to the German troops freeing them from the terror of the Russian Bolsheviks.

One day, Kārlis Pauļuks, a lawyer and later Minister of Justice for the Ulmanis government, came to St. Petersburg as a representative of the Latvian intelligentsia. Pauluks asked me if the occupation of Vidzeme was expected, and he was very happy when I gave him a definite confirmation, but I explained that the conquest of Latvia could not be guaranteed. He asked me to ask Keyserling what Latvians could expect after Germany's annexation of the country.

When I was able to announce Keyserling's answer on the next visit that no relocation or colonization was planned, Pauluks again looked very happy, for it seemed that he saw the opportunity to save the Latvian people from ceding land to Germany.

At the same time, the Latvians also held talks with the representatives of the Entente in St. Petersburg, represented by Mr. Seska. I learned of this through the former Permanent Secretary and, since the beginning of the war, the right-hand man of Foreign Minister Sazonov, Baron Moritz Schilling.

He contacted me to establish contacts with Keyserling and to talk about the rapid movement of the German army through Estonia to St. Petersburg. Schilling was a Russian-oriented monarchist, and hoped to liberate Russia from the Bolsheviks with the help of the Germans.

He regretted with a heavy heart that the price would be a separation of the Baltic provinces and their annexation to Germany. As one of his like-minded people, he mentioned the former Minister of Trade, Timirazev, who said that the efficient German management of the Baltic ports would be more beneficial to Russia than bad Russian supremacy.

Schilling presented to me his entire peace program for me to pass it on to Keyserling, emphasizing that it was infallible. However, the fact that he had discussed the programme with the ambassadors of the Entente considerably reduced the significance of the message. In addition, a peace agreement had to be reached for Germany to leave Belgium, and far-reaching negotiations on Alsace-Lorraine were needed, in exchange for Germany's desire to maintain its influence in the east.

The French and English ambassadors viewed the plan positively, but the Italian ambassador said: For our part, Germany can have eastern territories around the entire sea if we only get the Adriatic. When I pointed out to Mr Schilling that there was nothing to be done about the Alsace-Lorraine talks, he said:

"There will be tough fighting, but in the end the Germans will have to lower their sails."

I conveyed the main ideas from Schilling's statements to Keyserling, but I took his suggestions as a matter of course. At that time, no one in Germany thought about the cession of Alsace-Lorraine. Compared to the peace treaty signed a year later, this would be possible for Germany to emerge from the war brilliantly.

It is my conviction that then, after the collapse of Russia, when the importance of American aid had already begun, was the right moment for the Entente to agree to peace. Presumably, Germany, with the exception of Alsace-Lorraine, would have retained its territories and gained hegemony in the east. But the most important thing - a monarchy was to be preserved.

After the dissolution of the peace negotiations in Brest-Litovsk on February 20, 1918, the Germans launched an attack that in just a few days occupied all of Livonia and Estonia. I, with three other gentlemen, left St. Petersburg on the last train to Valka, which still stopped at Viru. We hid there for two days. The city had been occupied by Estonian communists, all German mansion owners and their families were arrested and taken away.

Our situation also became dangerous because we could be discovered at any time. On Sunday, February 24, there was a sudden relief. Thirteen soldiers from the German strike team had fled from Valka and released the prisoners. When eight more hussars and a combined army under the command of an Armenian major arrived a few hours later, the city fell completely into German hands after a brief massacre. Some red activists were arrested, some fled. The Russian cavalry squadron, which was retreating in the direction of Viru, was disarmed and allowed to continue its journey.

I learned from the Germans who had been in Cēsis that the Reds had arrested and taken many Germans there, including my sister-in-law, Rita Vietinghofff, who had been taking care of my children since my wife's death. So, I hurried along the sleigh road that led through Valka and Valmiera to Cēsis and my children. I was met by parts of the German army with different types of weapons, all in the best mood. A communist was hanging from the lamppost in Valka Square.

In 1918, the German occupation began with the best of hopes but ended in the worst disaster in Vidzeme's history.

I myself hoped that all my wishes would come true. The Diets, which were convened in March and July in joint with the neighbouring provinces, laid the foundation for the country's future political system. The members of the Knights, who had remained in Riga since 1917, under the leadership of Max Sievers, established close ties with the German Army High Command and saw the annexation of the Baltic States as a separate province to Prussia, the first step of which would be a union.

However, the idea provoked controversy in the Reichstag, but received majority support for the plan drawn up by Land Marshall, H. von Strick, for the formation of the Duchy of the Baltics, and the Duke of Mecklenburg, Adolph Friedrich Herzog zu Mecklenburg, was recommended for the post of duke and who also gave his consent.

I have only good memories of the German administration and the army people.

In the General Staff of Cēsis we had contact with a really intelligent, diligent officer, I knew Herr von Both and the Senator of Lübeck Neumann particularly well from the people of the administration. On several occasions, even in official matters, which reached the German Emperor, to whom I was grateful for the liberation of the country from the robbers, but especially for Germany's pressure on Russia to allow the return of our relatives whom the Reds had sent to Siberia.

The German soldiers who stayed with us at Straupe, mostly from Bavaria, behaved impeccably and gave us no reason to complain. Understandably during the war, with the circumstances of foreign military administrations present and partly because the German occupying forces did not always consult us sufficiently, we did not live completely without violence here either.

However, the reorganization of the administration, legislation, traffic and schools has been remarkably rapid, with some changes introduced. If the war had ended in a favourable way for Germany, the Baltic States could have flourished and developed under German leadership. Of course, the law would be based on Keyserling's pragmatic view: No Germanization of Estonians and Latvians, and no colonization. Unlike many of my friends, I was strongly opposed to the forced housing of German peasants in the Baltic States.

This could lead either to a long-standing tension between Germans and the local population or to the loss of the national identity of German farmers. History once decided that we, Balts, must be the foremost to serve Germany and our Baltic homeland by strengthening the necessary character traits. Strengthening this top tier with an influx from Germany will always be very welcome.

The breakdown came unexpectedly quickly. We were discussing the new constitution in Riga Castle when the news of the German emperor's abdication on November 9, 1918 came. Then events escalated. The German army units, taken over by the revolutionaries, left the Bolsheviks without a country. Only with great effort did Lieutenant Schmidt manage to secure the transportation of us Germans by rail to Riga from Cēsis - on December 23, 1918, Cēsis was occupied by the Bolsheviks. We hoped that we would be able to stay in Riga and feel safe

102

there on Christmas Eve. On January 23, 1919, Riga was occupied by the Bolsheviks. The city was filled with German troops. A few days ago, at a meeting at the House of Nobility, these concerns were called unfounded.

The city gave up unexpectedly easily. Within a few hours, I decided to take the opportunity to travel to Germany, a trip organized by an organization of knights, and on the morning of December 26, I went to Berlin with my six daughters and sister-in-law Rita Vietinghofff, where we arrived a day later.

On the way to the station in Pozen we had to witness the Poles disarming the German soldiers. In Berlin, everything was a mess. For a moment, it seemed as if the communists were going to come to power. We stayed near the Chancellor's Palace, in Michael's shelter on Wilhelmina Street. There was gunfire on the street all day. On Unter den Linden we could see sailors wandering around drunk, the old Berlin was no longer recognizable.

The marches of the Spartak Union created insecurity in the streets. By displaying inexhaustible heroism, the situation was saved by voluntary organizations formed by former officers. After the killings of Rosa Luxembourg and Karl Liebknecht, the Spartak movement was deprived of its leaders and the organization lost energy.

Coping was also difficult. At that time, we learned how much a person can be addicted to eating, even if we held back as much as we could. My eldest daughter was taken care of by the Baltischen Vertrauverband, two others of the children were accommodated in Mecklenburg and Schleswig, and the two youngest were taken to the Steglitz lyceum, (Steglitz is a district in the south of Berlin). Steglitz is densely built, and includes southern Berlin's largest shopping street, Schloss-strasse. In Steglitz, the cityscape transitions from the densely populated inner city to suburban areas with villas and single-family homes where my children and sister-in-law could move into a small apartment with the children.

I look for a job in vain. Sometimes I led the training of young Balts for the Landeswehr. When the struggle against the Bolsheviks had begun, they were sent to fight for their homeland. We watched with admiration their attacks in the most difficult conditions. The seat of the provincial council was in Liepaja, which was still in the hands of the German military administration, from where the Landeswehr and German troops also launched an attack. For the German formations, Count von Goltz was looking for volunteers in Berlin, and I have had the privilege of working with this great man on several occasions. The question arose as to whether and how the promises made to the people to recruit volunteers in the struggle could be fulfilled.

The future of the world was still uncertain. Land Marschall von Stryk, who was based in Stockholm, made it clear that the goal would be to establish a united Baltic state under an external protectorate. In November 1918, the government of the proclaimed Republic of Latvia was powerless in Liepaja, the Republic of Estonia functioned only thanks to the support of Finland, and the German-Baltic units fought against the Bolsheviks. Could they resist, that was the big question?

von Stryk's plans collapsed; they were too imaginative. He had to flee from Liepaja to Berlin when he was threatened with arrest, he had found articles that compromised the Latvian government. At the same time, he resigned from his position as Land Marschall. The day after my arrival, I met him in Berlin and, with the help of the Swedish envoy, tried to delay the extradition to the Latvians. I went to Szczecin to ask Pilar, who was supervising the sea route from Liepaja to Stockholm, to arrange contacts with a military agent in Stockholm, Nandschen, to try to obtain an exit document from Berlin to Sweden.

von Stryk had not lost his will to continue his political work, but felt that the chances of holding a position himself were unrealistic. Until the occupation of the Baltics by the Germans, he had many merits, as he provided the German military leadership with valuable information and various documents that facilitated the preparation of the attack. In Berlin, he learned how to make extensive useful contacts and played a prominent role in political life as a representative of the Baltic states.

After the elections to Land Marschall, Stryk often took an opposing position to the supreme army commander, and he was usually right, especially in his opposition to the annexation of the Baltic States to Prussia. He was the first to warn against overly optimistic forecasts already in the summer. Stryk had always taken a national German position. That is why it made me all the sadder at his transition to the Entente, in which we could not believe. Later, Stryk completely renounced all public engagement. While I, like many others who lived in the German countryside, got to know the hospitality of the German farmers, the news of the Liepāja coup came, which led to Pastor Niedra becoming Prime Minister instead of Ulmanis, who together with the German-Baltic countries set up a Council of Ministers.

Lielstraupe Castle 1930

A few weeks later we received good news in that the German Landeswehr (Land Defence) had occupied Riga on 22 May.

The city, which was very well armed, was captured by a small group of heroes who, via the wide bridges, crossed the river in a frontal attack. The message echoed throughout Europe. Two days later I arrived in Magdeburg and in a café on the front page of the French newspaper Temps (Time) I saw a statement written in large letters: La prize de Riga per la troupe de secousse balte. Manteuffel tué an cours de la prize de Riga.

A few days later I arrived in Riga with some other gentlemen. The joy of being free from the dangers of the Bolshevik government was overshadowed by the pain of those killed on the battlefield and many were those killed by the red animals. Among the latter was also my best friend - Baltazar Campenhausen.

106

Full of anxiety and worry, I received the news of the conflict between the Landeswehr and Estonians. After occupying Riga, the Landeswehr near Cēsis had clashed with Estonian troops, who, together with the Latvian military units loyal to the Ulmani government, liberated the country from the Bolsheviks heading north.

Instead of finding a warring party among the Estonians, as expected, the Landeswehr was subjected to a hostile attack. Gunfire broke out, the landowner was occupied by Cēsis. Niedra's government declared war on Estonia, but at the same time appealed for mediation with the Entente. The German High Command, of which the Landeswehr was also a part, demanded the immediate withdrawal of the Estonian army, but the Estonians refused.

The talks in Cēsis on 10 June ended with the unanimous decision of the representatives of the United States, England and France that the Estonians should leave the territory of Latvia by 1 July. A ceasefire was proclaimed for a week, at the end of which the plenipotentiaries of both parties had to arrive at Cēsis to conclude the peace.

We in Riga looked forward to a future solution to the conflict. We learned from Landeswehr circles that the fight against Estonians had not become popular.

However, the Estonians took advantage of the truce to bring more troops here. On the agreed day, no Estonian arrived for the planned peace treaty negotiations.

The German commander-in-chief, Count Golz, received an order from Reval/Tallinn from the English general Gough to withdraw his troops to the territory west of Lielstraupe. All Latvian ministers from the Cabinet of Ministers of Niedra recommended organizing a new attack and expelling the Estonians, because, according to their intelligence service, their combat capacity was very limited.

The German High Command, indignant at the breach of promise and English vanity, agreed. Within a few days, they planned to reach the land border near Valka. Niedra hoped for supporters from northern Latvia, and elections would take place immediately after the expulsion of the Estonians, in which he intended to gain support for his government.

At that time, we considered the Estonians to be allies of the Bolsheviks, and with their hostility towards the Germans, they certainly lived up to this.

We also hoped for the political support of the Entente, which had ordered the Estonians to withdraw their troops by 1 July.

A leading group, called the Iron Division, was in alliance with the Germans involved in the Landeswehr, they did not question the loyalty of their troops. However, the soldiers remained in Riga for several weeks, during which time the army gave in to demoralizing encouragement. The soldiers thought they had found a place to live here, they did not understand the meaning of the new battle and could not carry it out. The Landeswehrs most valuable task force was withdrawn to Riga.

A little about the battles near Cēsis and Lielstraupe. My old aunt Emilija Rosen stayed here and during the shooting she moved to the castle's basement with a country kitchen. She experienced the departure of the Iron Division and the attack of the Estonians, which caused her courage to drop and she remained completely terrified.

At first, the Landeswehr made quite significant progress, but had to retreat. As for the artillery armament, the Estonians were in a much stronger position, they used English weapons and English soldiers also fought among them to secure their position. Within days, the Estonians were near Riga, where a

German force with rarely seen heroism delayed them at Lake Jugla, until negotiations began, ending with a ceasefire agreement signed at Strazdi Manor.

As a result of the pressure from the Entente, the representatives agreed that the German troops would leave Riga, the Estonian units would not enter the city, only the Latvian army went there. The Niedra government resigned and Ulmanis regained his seat.

During the talks, along with a large part of the members of Congress, I left Riga because it was to be expected that Estonians, together with their Latvian friends, could occupy Riga and then start murdering and robbing. After the departure of the German soldiers and the Landeswehr, the return of the Bolsheviks could not be ruled out.

Gersdorf remained in Riga and wanted to start negotiations with the Latvians.

I went to Berlin, but for two weeks I also visited Tilzīte/Tilsit, from where I returned, having expected news from my home country. The train went to Jelgava, which was still in German hands, from there I took a boat to Riga. A few weeks later, I went to Straupe, where I had to apply for permission for the first time from a farmer who was the commander.

My return to the manor proved to be successful, as I managed to take over the management of the Lielstraupe manor again and, until the confiscation in October 1920, was able to earn income from the forest, which later made life easier, since all previous cash savings had been lost due to a monetary reform. I experienced critical days in Lielstraupe in October 1919, when parts of the Bermont army moved as far as Torņakalns. The Latvian government fled to Cēsis and had to reckon with the retreat of Latvian troops.

I went to the forest to the forester Germann, but returned two days later, for I learned in Cēsis that Bermonts attack had been stopped. A few weeks later, while I was in town, I experienced a senseless shooting.

The following winter, I made contacts with the American and British military and diplomatic representatives, who showed us Balts sympathy, even though we could not count on any help. Missionary representatives who were hostile to the Baltic States were soon replaced. Even the English commander Alexander, who had been a landowner since the Treaty of Peace in Strazdu Manor, could not prevent these proud parts from being transformed into the infantry regiment of Tukum, dressed in Latvian army uniforms and appointing a Latvian commander. The Latvian state was consolidated. Only once, around Christmas 1920, did the Bolsheviks seem to be in danger of an invasion. But everything remained calm. Over time, more and more Baltic Germans who had fled to Germany returned. I took my family back in 1920.

My brother Voldemar's widow Elza took over the management of the farm, my sister-in-law Rita Viettinghof stayed in Steglitz with my youngest children until 1923 and then went to her brothers and sisters in Schwerin, because the country had become lawless.

After a short time in Riga, I received an official request to become the chairman of the credit committee and advisor to the Vidzeme Nobles Credit Union, thus I got a beautiful official residence there in 1920/1921. In the winter of that year, I was often visited by acquaintances, especially those who lived in the countryside. Here you could find the social cohesion needed in difficult times. In the autumn of 1921, the credit union, which had been so successful for a long time, was wound up on the orders of the Latvian government and its property was confiscated, thus terminating my activities.

The liquidation of the Vidzeme Landlords Credit Union was an event in a chain carried out by the Latvian government, to reduce the economic and political power of the large landowners. The culmination was the law of 20 September 1920 on the agrarian reform. According to it, the land was confiscated to be allocated to the landless, leaving only fifty hectares to the original owner. The fact that the forest was also confiscated was a clear demonstration of the state's desire to eliminate the welfare of the gentry, reduce their influence and support itself on its own. The need for reforms was already recognized by the knights themselves, who submitted several important proposals to the Latvian government, which, in order to satisfy the urgent desire for land, proposed the formation of special associations.

I was convinced that the government would not allow itself to be influenced (which it did not) and in February-May 1920 I opposed further agricultural proposals. However, the majority of the Convention took the position - animam salvari. The catastrophe - its implementation throughout the country - could not be prevented. The bills, where we could see compensation at first, were later amended, on the initiative of the left, frightened by the outrage of the people. We had only a few profitable remnants of land, it would be wrong to use the name - mansion.

For me, personal disputes about my house and mansion were handled with Latvian officials. The Lielstraupe parish, with whom I have had good relations for many years, sent a formal request to the government to leave all my property at my disposal for at least a few more years, accompanied by a covering letter with 750 signatures. The consequence was that my property was not expropriated. First of all, I was left with our old castle, where we spent our summers regularly. It was a gathering point for the family and a German meeting centre in Vidzeme.

Two repurchased farms, which I was first allowed to keep, were to be sold according to an amendment to the law. The house that I built myself, where I lived with my wife and children for eleven years, was also confiscated, our summer cottage in Saulkrasti met the same fate. If I did not receive a salary as a member of the Kredītbanka Council and a member of the Board of Directors of the limited liability company Landmann (formerly Liepāja Farmers Consumer Association Selbsthilfe), my family could not be supported. This was the situation for all manor owners. No one could live on income that did not exist. Perhaps it could be possible to survive by working in cities or having other incomes. I had lost all hope of an improved situation.

We complained about the injustice of the League of Nations. This step was recommended by German farmers to us. At the beginning, we were still hesitant, because we wanted to get support from all the Baltic German countries, we also had to wait for an opportune moment. This came at a time when any compensation was irrevocably rejected.

In the first, consultative body of the League of Nations, our legal opinion was recognized as correct, but the matter met with no further success, because the Latvian government imagined in an imaginative way the dangers of Bolshevism that might arise if the conditions of the agrarian reform were changed. As before, we asserted the right to compensation and brought an action before the Hague Court.

Our representative in this campaign was Deputy Baron Fircks who, with the help of Berlin's specialist on minorities, Dr. Bruhn's tips, was the best advisor. I also had the opportunity to talk to this wonderful person about these issues. If we are lucky, we can succeed. Legal recognition of our views would further strengthen the political position and prestige, even if it was still high enough in rural areas. The respect and trust we enjoy prove that we have treated the people of the country fairly. In the future, if the purchase of land is allowed, I hope to increase the impossible part with the help of cheap loans, thus ensuring the possibility of existence in the mansion.

The knights of Vidzeme had already met a similar fate as the large landowners. In the autumn of 1919, I reconstructed the meeting of the nobility.

Since the members of our association lived abroad, we elected for the remaining members of the country deputies from the nobles in accordance with the law of order. Gersdorf, Lantråd, took the lead and stayed in place. After the resignation of the former Marshal von Stryk, elected by the Diet in 1918, and the resignation of the former Marshal of the Land, Baron Pilar, who served as deputy, moved to Germany, the Convention elected me as Deputy Land Marschall.

Shortly before the conclusion, there was a lively discussion in the Parliament. It was clear that the Latvian government was planning to dismantle the knightly organization. Most of the knightly house had already been removed. Several members of the Convention, first and foremost our archivist H. von Bruiningk, feared that an association of Latvians and nobility could be formed on the Finnish model without any political rights, limited by legislation. I fought against this plan because it meant the dissolution of Vidzeme chivalry.

The idea also did not receive the consent of the majority of the convention. In April 1920, as Deputy Land Marschall, I presided over the last meeting of the knighthood of Vidzeme. It was held in the Landrats Room of the Knights House, with about 75 gentlemen in attendance. The Diet decided, among other things, to grant voting rights to landowners who did not retain their property. Subsequently, it was decided that, in the event of the cessation of chivalry, its property and management of the foundations should be entrusted to the Vidzeme General Society (Livländischen Gemeinnützigen Verband), which we had recently set up and asked the government to approve as a legal representative. What we were afraid of happened. In June 1920, when an ad hoc law was passed, the Latvian Parliament decided to abolish the knighthood of Vidzeme and Kurzeme, followed by the dismissal of legal entities.

The convent of the nobility, chaired by the then Landrat von Strandman, met again to express its displeasure and protest.

After that, the Knights of Vidzeme ceased to exist as a public institution with state functions.

But its traditions, which no power in the world could deprive her, were further inherited by the Vidzeme General Society, whose task was to unite all Vidzeme nobles. Tasks related to the management of the knightly heritage, the maintenance of family records, the promotion of the knightly culture, especially from a historical point of view. But above all, there was concern for the integrity of members of knights' organizations. In one of the assignments subordinated to the Society, I paved the way for the publication of a book, which, according to my suggestion, was still referred to as "the last convent of knights." The purpose of the publication was to reflect the importance of chivalry for the development of our country from a scientific and historical point of view. This knightly monument was promised to be created by Dr. A. von Tobien, whom we had been the last man to occupy in our noble matrix in the Convention.

In keeping with tradition, members of the former noble Congress were elected to the Council of the General Society. Having previously been Deputy Land Marschall, I had been given the presidency which I still hold. I consider it my duty to take care of and keep alive the ancient spirit of Vidzemes' chivalry, in close connection with the Verband des Livländischen Stammadels, which unites representatives of the nobility in Germany and which I regularly attend in Berlin. At our last meeting in May of this year, which was attended by 230

representatives of chivalry, it gave us great hope and confirmed our spiritual
strength. May it survive all the storms of the future!

Lielstraupe, august 1926

Baron Hans Rosen

Poznan i Poland

Hans von Rosen left Latvia after the Russians occupied the Baltic
States in 1940 and settled in Germany-occupied Poland. When Germany
invaded Poland in 1939, properties were taken over by Germans who
had moved in. The area had previously been German until WWI as part
of Prussia but was returned to Poland with the Treaty of Versailles. This
resulted in the German population in the eastern parts (East Prussia
with Königsberg (today's Kaliningrad)) being cut off from the motherland. Between WWI and WWII, the Germans had tried to establish a
connection between East Prussia and the motherland but had not succeeded. Earlier German populations had been forced out or subjugated
by the Poles between WWI and WWII and when the Germans invaded
Poland in 1939, these properties were retaken by the Germans. Who assigned to whom the different estates? Johann von Rosen must have been
assigned by someone and what happened to the previous family? Did
they get the property back in 1945 when the Germans were pushed back
against Germany? The name of the estate that Johan von Rosen and his
family moved into was Sierniki (Gut Wegheim) and was owned by the
Mieczkowski family.

There were a lot of families that were affected. What were their fates?
Did they get their farms and estates back or did they remain confiscated
(which I think they were)?

HANS VON ROSEN UPPSALA, SVERIGE (HVR)

HvR lived in Uppsala when I spoke to him in 2013. I had written him a letter and asked some general questions about the family and he called me up and we talked a little about what life was like in the Baltics. He also mentioned that it was quite common for the barons to sow their wild oats at that time.

Sowing wild oats is something that has always existed in all social classes, so nothing unique really. When we talked about the Brüsewitz family, he mentioned that they might have come from Russia. He drew an example of a Russian tsarina who had come from Denmark but did not want to boast about it.

HvR further said that Hans Johann Otto von Rosen had been present when HvR graduated in 1943.

HvR had left his Lyckholm estate in Noarootsi in western Estonia in 1939 to start studying at the University of Agricultural Sciences in Danzig. In 1951 he moved to Uppsala in Sweden and the University of Agricultural Sciences. He also told me that his oldest son is a professor of statistics there if I remember correctly. His wife was buried in Estonia. Most Baltic Germans came to the Poznan area (Warthegau) and not to Danzig as the HvR did after they left Estonia.

He also said that the Swedish time was not as good as has been claimed. The peasants were taxed very heavily in many ranks by the various landlords. Before the Swedish era, the peasants only paid tribute to the church, which in itself meant that the priests could live as landlords.

ALEXANDER HERZEN (1812 - 1870)

Alexander Herzen[25] was born in Moscow in 1812 and died in Paris in 1870.

He was the son of a Russian nobleman, Ivan Yakovlev, and a German woman from Stuttgart, Luise Haag. They were married during a Lutheran wedding ceremony, which was not approved in Russia, so the child, Alexander, lived as an illegitimate son. The name Herzen was invented by his parents as he could not bear his father's name. Russia was a country with mainly Russian Orthodox religious faith.

Alexander Ivanovich Herzen is your first cousin twice removed's husband's first cousin twice removed's great niece's husband's grandfather.

| Du | → | Felix Virro
your father | → | Marie Helene Elisabeth Wirro
his mother | → | Johannes Ludvig August Brüsewitz
her father | → | Elise Amalie Caroline Madsen
his sister |

Dagmar Susanne von Ungern-Sternberg — her daughter → Viktor von Ungern-Sternberg — her husband → Nicolai Constantin von Ungern-Sternberg — his father →

Freiherr Fredrik Adolf * von Ungern-Sternberg — his father → Augusta Magdalena von Rosen — his mother → Robert Fabian von Rosen — her brother →

Камилла Романовна = София Романовна von Rosen — his daughter → Андрей Васильевич Каншин — her husband → Аполлинария Васильевна Лазарева — his sister →

Зинаида Васильевна Стопица — her daughter → Nina Evgenevna Herzen — her daughter → Pyotr Alexandrovich Herzen — her husband → Alexander Alexandrovich Herzen — his father

→ Alexander Ivanovich Herzen — his father

But surnames are rarely used in Russian society, so he was called his and his father's baptismal name, Alexander Ivanovich.

Alexander Herzen's socialist views were considered completely new in Germany at the time and were almost completely ignored in the new literature. Alexander was expelled from Russia after being exiled within the kingdom first, and he settled in Paris. There he became friends with James Rothschild, from the highly influential banking family, who also helped Alexander to transfer part of his wealth from Russia. Maybe it should be that you need to be rich to be able to think free thoughts, the others were busy getting food on the table.

---

[25] More info and pictures are available at: https://en.wikipedia.org/wiki/Alexander_Herzen

The Rothschild banking family in France is a French banking dynasty founded in 1812 in Paris by James Mayer de Rothschild (1792–1868). James was sent there from his home in Frankfurt, Germany, by his father, Mayer Amschel Rothschild (1744–1812).

THE BRÜSEWITZ FAMILY IN THE BALTIC STATES

The Brüsewitz family

It may have been that the Brüsewitz family had been recruited by Count von Sievers, who owned the estate (Wilsenhof/Vilzeni in Livonia where Hermann worked. In the mid-1800s, the old peasant society was on its way out and industrialism was at the door. The count probably saw the business opportunities in this early on and began to mine peat for heating factories and homes, as well as the use of bricks as building materials for factories and homes.

After moving to Tallinn, Hermann settled on the Jälgimäe estate, which was owned by Alexander Nikolai von Glehn. Hermann's son Johannes (my grandmother's "stepfather") had also lived at Jälgimäe but moved to Vardi in 1902. Johannes had married Marri in 1893; she was a housekeeper at Vardi for Max Pilar von Pilchau. The question is whether Marri lived at Vardi without her husband from 1893 to 1902? What will the relationship be with the children that Marri had and Johannes?

The local Estonian population reportedly had no experience of this, and labour had to be recruited from Pomerania.

The peasants in Estonia at this time were given passports and could later begin to move freely within the country and could also take work in the factories. Serfdom had been abolished, which made it possible for the population to move within the country and seek various jobs.

The Hermann Brüsewitz family seem to have come to Estonia via Livonia from Prussia, but it is still unclear from where in Prussia. In Polish, the name Brüsewitz is BRUDZEWICE.

There are also two villages in Poland of the same name, one in central Poland (region Łódź) and one in the northwest (Szczecin). In Germany, there is a town called Brüsewitz. I've tried to connect one of these towns or villages with the family but so far, I've failed to do so.

MIGRATION

My grandmother's mother was married into a German family, Brüsewitz. After being able to follow the family from Livonia to Estonia, the traces of the family emigrating to Wolhynia, in connection with WW1, end.

There is uncertainty about the year in which Hermann and his wife moved to Livonia. The fact that Hermann and his wife Hanna Caroline Wilhelmine, née Kasch, had their first child Carl in 1862 does not mean that they moved there then.

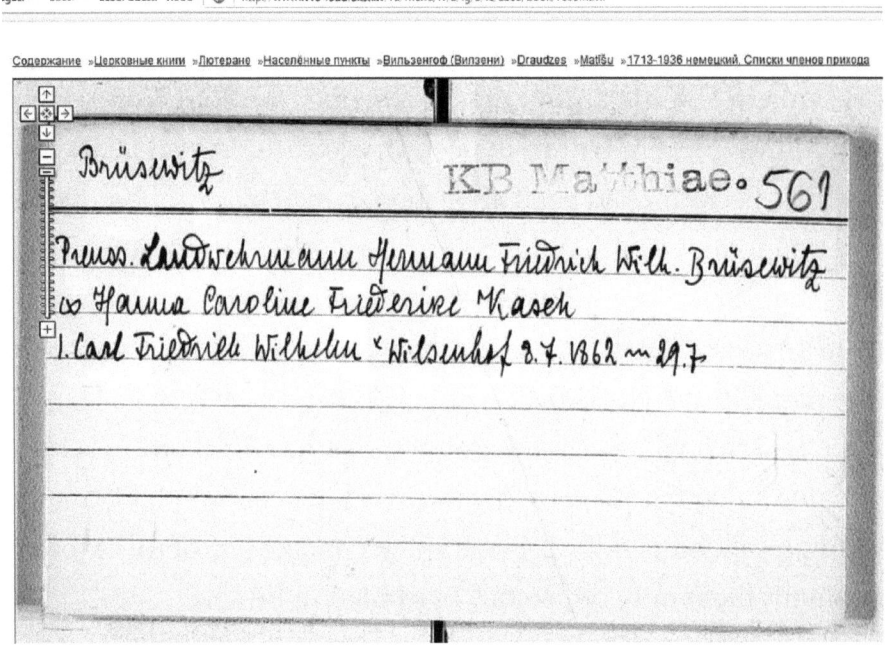

Carl Friedrich Wilhelm Brüsewitz

It is stated here that Hermann was a Prussian Landwehrmann, while there are reports where he is listed as a brick burner and peat miner.

It may have happened before. If they came via Prussia, they had to pass through Lithuania. Perhaps they came via Russia, as one person had suggested?

When an archive source in a church book states that a person has his or her background in Prussia, no village or town mentioned, how should one act? The different areas that are relevant are large and difficult to search in.

The following archival information for Hermann states:

Brüsewitz, Hermann † 5.1.1908 in Maksimowka, Sohn von Johann Brüsewitz, Alter 71 Jahre und 11 Monate, verheiratet, gebürtig aus Preußen.

(Quelle: Ev.luth. Kirchenbuch Heimtal 1908 Verstorbene, S. 179, Nr. 206 im Staatsarchiv Shitomir Fond 67/8/5)

WOLHYNIA (UKRAINE)

The German settlements to this area were not organized on state initiative but on private ones. The migration was encouraged by local nobles, often Polish landowners, who wanted to develop their significant land holdings in the area for agriculture. Wolhynia was part of what is today western Ukraine, the area west of Kiev up to the Polish border.

In some literature, it can be read that this move to Wolhynia would have been a result of the Russian Tsarina Catherine II issuing a decree in 1763, but more recent research has shown through Dr. Mikhaylo Kostiuk from 2012 that this is incorrect. The decree applied to other parts of Russia, but not to Wolhynia, which was then still part of Poland.

The landowners had lost their cheap labour when serfdom was abolished, and therefore advertised in Poland and Germany for tenants and buyers of land willing to move to the area. An acre of land could then be purchased for ten to sixteen Rubles.

However, it was often forest and swamp land that had to be cleared and drained, which required extensive work. The rented land eventually became the tenant's property.

The governor of Wolhynia, in a report in 1887, expressed his resignation over the following state of affairs. Colonists mixed mainly with Jews; They had almost no relations with the peasants and treated them with contempt. A German colonist never married a peasant woman, and a German woman never married a peasant. The proximity between colonies and settlements led to hostility between peasants and colonists.

The two main factors that attracted German colonists to Wolhynia were the Russian agrarian reform of 1861 and the Polish uprising of 1863.

The abolition of serfdom deprived Wolhynian landowners of their cheap access to agricultural labour and political instability in the Vistula region and subsequent uprisings, causing thousands of German colonists to emigrate from Poland. Wolhynia was not densely populated at that time and a lot of cheap untouched land was available. The territory was well suited for colonization.

The attractiveness of Wolhynia to German emigrants from the Polish kingdom and German lands was also largely due to its territory's geographical proximity to the Polish governorates. According to the Ministry of Internal Affairs, which based its report on data from inspectors of the Kiev Education District, there were at least 373 German schools in

Wolhynia in 1887. Sixty of these were located in Pastor Johanson's Evangelical Lutheran congregation Heimtal, 113 could be found in Pastor Kerm's Rozhyshche congregation and more than 200 in Pastor Wasem's Zhytomyr congregation. The highest number, 392 schools, was noted by Brockhaus and Efron's Encyclopaedia in 1891. German schools made up one-fifth of all schools in the governor's office.

By the end of the 19th century, Wolhynia had more than 200,000 German settlers.

The vast majority of these Germans were Protestant Lutherans. A limited number of Mennonites from the lower region of the Vistula River settled in the southern part of Wolhynia. Baptists and Moravian brethren settled mostly northwest of Zhitomir.

It is interesting that in Estonia a parish called Heimtal was formed in southern Estonia west of the town of Võru, adjacent to the Sömerpalu estate. There were about 35 - 40 families that emigrated from Heimdal, Ukraine to Heimdal in Estonia between 1907 - 1915.

The reason was said to be that there was plenty of work in Estonia as the first failed Bolshevik revolution of 1905/06 had eroded the confidence of the German landlords in the local workers.

The Brüsewitz family in Wolhynia

The capital of the Brüsewitz family was Heimtal, close to the current city of Zhytomyr in Ukraine, which was then called Shitomir by the Germans.

Dorothea Elisabeth Julie Brüsewitz (1866 - ?)

Dorothea Elisabeth Julie Brüsewitz

Born 09.02.1866 in Kambi (Campen), Harju-Jaani parish. She married Michael Zittlau on 28.07.1893 in Tallinn, Niguliste.

Michael worked as a blacksmith in Tallinn in 1893 and after they had moved to Wolhynia he worked as a Küsterlehrer in the Wolhynische Küsterschule in the district of Zhitomir in 1929.

If you look at a direct translation of Küster, it is in English sixteen, which in turn means bell-ringer, church caretaker. Perhaps they were also cantors when the level of education for Wolhynian cantors was low. These cantors not only worked as teachers, but in the absence of the pastor they were also representatives of the spiritual authority of the village and were therefore often religious. Perhaps they had tasks such as bell ringers and gravediggers as well.

An interesting link to read more about life in Wolhynia:

https://www.myvolyn.de/wolhynien-spezial/luth-kirche-russland-1909.html

Children of Dorothea Brüsewitz and Michael Zittlau:

Emil Ernst Zittlau was born in 1901 in the village of Tatartschek, Zhytomyr, Wolhynia, and died in 1985 in Berlin. He married Lydia Henkelmann in 1929 in Rhein, Kreis Lötzen.

Marie Julie Amalie Brüsewitz (1876 - ?)

Hermanns daughter, Marie Julie Amalie Brüsewitz, was born in 1876 in Rasik/Raasiku.

Godparents: Gräfin E. v. Sievers, Frl. Julie Müller, A. Diedrichs.

She married the widower Henrich Timnik who had 3 children with him into the marriage.

They married in 1898 in Geytmalsky Parish Church in Zhitomir County, Volyn Province.

Together they had 3 children:

Marie did not like a tough farm life and began to run away and left for good in 1907.

The man Marie had started dating was a Ukrainian bookkeeper from Kiev, Felix Jurkovski.

The last known address for Marie was Tatarskaya Str 1 in Kiev in 1914, which was probably Felix's address.

Timnick began a divorce process that lasted for 7 years until 1913, when the divorce was finalized. The archive material in St. Petersburg is a huge chunk of 150 documents.

WWI then started and the tracks disappeared.

Pastor Julius Hermann Johannson (1852 – 1917)

Pastor Johanson[26] from Heimtal, not satisfied with the knowledge and skills of his teachers, tried to create a training centre for them in order to improve their professional skills and cultural understanding. He subscribed to newspapers and sent them to the schools of teachers and colonists to inform them and broaden their views. A pastor had to be a baptized and confirmed man, at least 25 years old, have graduated from the Faculty of Theology of Yuryiv (Derpt/Dorpat/Tartu) University, and also have passed the University Board exam. He had to master four languages (Russian, German, Latin and Greek) and had to master one

---

[26] Julius Hermann Johannson was a relative on my maternal grandfather's side in Estonia

Russian subject. Pastors were highly educated people. They received a salary from the state treasury and they were paid to perform religious ceremonies and rituals. Congregation members took care of their properties and gardens, providing them with fuel and grain.

96 pastors controlled and directed the life of their congregations and were particularly important in the education system within their congregation.

An excerpt from a local article in Heimtal told the story of the young teacher Eduard Schulz, who lived in East Wolhynia, and his search for a bride. He had an ideal of what a sixteen-teacher's wife should be like in terms of education, character, and appearance. One person he thought of was Pastor Johannson's wife.

Quote from the article: *The vicar's wife Friederike Johannson, who was always able to give a detailed answer to all questions that the farmers of the parish turned to the pastorate about during the time when the vicar was absent. He often praised her in his diary. She proved her enormously high level of competence and passionate enthusiasm for her husband's career choice, even when Mr. Pastor was suddenly arrested in 1915, before the forced move.*

Nothing deterred her. At night, without witnesses, she and her three minor children secretly carried church equipment and supplies and about 15,000 books from the seminary and church library to a hiding place, thus saving Heimtal parish treasures from disappearing during the years of rebellion.

WWI

August Kork (1887 - 1937)

A relative on my grandmother's side through her partner Jaan Märtin was August Kork[27].

August Kork was born in 1887 in Haaslava Vangi (prison). His mother was Liis Kork, father unknown.

In 1908, August graduated from the Chuguev Military School, and in 1914 from the Nikolai General Staff Academy in St. Petersburg.

He continued at the school and trained reconnaissance pilots/observers. During WWI, he fought in the Tsarist army and advanced to official at the army headquarters on the Western Front.

From 1917 to 1918 he was chairman of the Committee for the Military of the Western Front.

From 1918 to 1019, August served in the Operations Department of the Red Army headquarters.

From December 1918 to June 1919, he served the Estonian Workers' Commune, formally a puppet state of Soviet Russia, as a consultant to the People's War Commissariat and later Chief of Staff of the so-called Municipal Army, which led the struggle for the Red Army fighting against the Republic of Estonia.

---

[27] More info and pictures are available at: https://en.wikipedia.org/wiki/August_Kork

In the summer of 1919, he was commander of the Red Army's Seventh Army.

In 1919, he led the defence of Petrograd against General Nikolai Yudenich.

He was commander of the 15th Army in 1919–20, he participated in the war against Poland.

He was the commander of the Sixth Army, in 1920–21 he fought against Peter Wrangel's troops in Ukraine and Crimea, and led the attack on the Perekop Isthmus, as a result of which Crimea surrendered to the Red Army and ended the Russian Civil War.

From 1921 to 1922, he was the head of the Kharkov Military District and deputy commander of the Soviet Ukrainian Armed Forces.

In 1922–23 he was commander of the Turkestan front and fought against the local resistance movement, Basmatchis.

From 1923 to 1928, he was commander of various military districts and the Caucasian army.

From 1928 to 1929 he was military attaché for the Soviet Union in Germany.

From 1929 to 1935, he was the commander of the Moscow Military District.

From 1935 to 1937 he was a member of the Council of the People's Commissariat of Defence and head of the M. Frunze Military Academy.

In 1927 he joined the Communist Party and from 1935 he was an army commander of the 2nd rank (colonel general).

In 1957, he was rehabilitated due to lack of the necessary evidence.

His schoolmates in this academy were also (later Estonian generals) Johan Laidoner (1912) and Jaan Soots (1913), who in 1917 invited A. Kork to join the new Estonian army.

Kork didn't want to take the risk and decided to become a teacher, thinking of abandoning his military career altogether. Perhaps there was no position (status) in the small Estonian army that was good enough for him.

Kork had married in 1914 to a Russian widow named Ekaterina Mihhailovna (maiden name unknown), who had high ambitions that made A. Kork decide to join the Red Army in 1918.

August Cork with wife

Kork was executed as a traitor in 1937, his wife as a terrorist in 1941. His contemporaries had different opinions about his past lifestyle and political views.

There are those who believe that with Stalin purged his most meritorious military personnel, it took a while before the war machine began to work when Hitler attacked the Soviet Union.

See The military trials in Moscow in 1937.

130

During the Stalinist purges, he was accused of organizing an armed conspiracy within the Red Army in 1937 and was shot.

Voronezh

Carl Friedrich Wilhelm Brüsewitz (1862 – 1925)

Carl was born in 1862 in Vilzeni (Wilsenhof), LAT S:t Matthias, Wolmar, and died in 1925 in Viljandi, Estonia.

His first wife was Bertha Caroline Tõnnisson, from Tallinn, born in 1861.

They married in 1892 at home.

Bertha died of tuberculosis before 1906 (Tallinn?).

Together they had a son, Gerhard Hermann Manfred Brüsewitz, born in 1895, Tallinn Oleviste; died in 1911, only 16 years old.

After Bertha's death, Carl remarried to Ann Kauber. She was born in 1877.

They married in 1907 in the church in Viljandi

On September 12, 1939, Ann changed her surname Brüsewitz to Priivitz. During Estonia's independent period between the two world wars, many of the population wanted to get rid of their German-sounding names.

Children of Carl Brüsewitz and Ann Kauber:

- Helene Miralda (Yelena) Brüsewitz, born 1913, Pärsti near Viljandi; died 1915, only 1 year old.

He worked as a forester in 1892 in Estonia and later until his death as a tailor, first in Germany and later in Estonia.

In the autumn of 1914, he was deported (as a German) from Viljandi to Voronezh in southwestern Russia, not far from the border with Ukraine. In 1920, after his deportation, he chose to go to Germany to work as a tailor.

In 1922, he was given permission to return to Estonia and worked as a tailor there as well.

World War I was the first time Russia went to war against Germany since the Napoleonic era, and Germans living in Russia were quickly suspected of sympathizing with enemy Germany. Many of these Germans were banished from the European part of Russia by the Tsarist government as enemies of the state - generally without any trial or any evidence.

The background to this deportation can be read in the book "Germans of the Soviet Union", by Irina Mukhina.

Ann (as the wife of a German) was so frightened that she left the Lutheran Church and both she and her young daughter converted to the "Russian Tsar's religion" - in 1915 in the Orthodox Church in Viljandi.

Carl had to leave his wife behind in Estonia when he was exiled to Voronezh.

After Ann and Carl lost their daughter Helena Miralda in 1915 to pneumonia, she worked as a housekeeper/housewife in Tallinn and Pärnu.

Carl was exiled to Voronezh and could not be present when his daughter died.

From 1920 to 1922 Carl lived in the district of Stallupönen, Eydtkuhnen, Memelland, Prussia (which was part of Germany).

132

Carl received Estonian citizenship in 1924. He was the only one of Hermann's children to have Estonian citizenship.

Carl died on 11.10.1925 in Viljandi, EST Jaani, Viljandi and he was buried in Viljandi, Estonia on 14.10.1925.

The cause of death was pleuritis, he was 63 years old.

Saratov

The deportation to Saratov in the Cossack-dominated area with the various factions of the Cossacks' loyalty to the Tsar was put to the test when the revolution broke out in October 1917.

How were the colonists handled? The northern parts of the Don Cossack territory were loyal to the Tsar, while the workers were supported by the Bolsheviks.

The southern parts of the Cossack territory in the Ukraine were also supported by the propertied larger landowners with the help of the Whites, the Tsar's soldiers.

The workers who supported the ideas of the revolution were also supported by the Jews, and innumerable battles broke out in the steppe landscapes of the Cossacks west and south on the Don River.

The Cossacks were a people who had escaped the grip of the serf-tsar and made a home for themselves on the great plains around the Don. They valued their freedom highly.

To then be deported as the colonists were to this area during WWI cannot have been easy.

How were the colonists treated during the war and the revolution.

When the counter-revolution began, most of the colonists were released from their exile and they returned home to their farms in Ukraine.

The farms were heavily looted and destroyed, but they restored their farms only to be forced to flee again after the counter-revolution was repulsed.

The Don Cossacks

The Cossacks were a people who fled their role as serfs in Russia and who in connection with this were given the name Cossacks. They settled in the river delta on the Don River, on the west side.

During World War I, they were loyal to the Tsar of Russia and stood on the side of the White Army in the fight against the German and Hungarian-Austrian armies.

When the revolution broke out in October 1917, they began to waver in their loyalty to the tsar. They were landowners themselves and there was a fear that they would also lose their land, but they had a hard time fighting their Russian brothers and they were faced with a difficult choice when it came to the idea of the counter-revolution that was planned and where the Cossacks were asked to side with the old power elite in this struggle.

It was also a desperate attempt to maintain their old privileges of the officers. Many of the Cossacks were quite uneducated, but they were not stupid, on the contrary, they possessed good common sense.

The propaganda from the frightening Social Democratic movement became intense on the battlefields, but the Cossacks were mostly war-weary and wanted to go home to their families on their farms on the Don.

From the revolution in October 1917 to the end of the war in 1918, things got quite messy in the ranks to complete the war.

The counter-revolution that started after the revolution lasted until 1922 before it was finally crushed by the Bolsheviks.

In the counter-revolution that followed the revolution, many people who had previously been family members and friends were pitted against each other. Something that also happened later in Estonia during WWII. Boys from the same villages could fight on either side, one on the side of the Bolsheviks and one on the side of the Germans.

In the same way as during the Second World War, when the boys in the villages of Estonia could be pitted against each other on different sides of the war, it had also been in Russia with the Don Cossacks.

When the resistance to the Red Army diminished and finally ceased, there was a shortage of many basic goods that the Soviet power could not provide to its citizens.

When the Reds gained power in the Don district, there was a shortage of almost everything. The Soviet power could not supply its citizens with soap, sugar, salt, kerosene, matches, Machorka or wagon lubricant.

Instead of burning kerosene, butter and lard were used in their kerosene lamps.

They also had to resort to a new-old method as an alternative to the matches when they had to use flint and kindlers to get a fire. The wicks were boiled in water with sunflower seed ash so that when they dried, they would ignite more easily. Despite this, it was not easy anyway.

When the Cossacks were going to roll themselves a cigarette, there was no paper, so they went into the pastor's office and snatched the church books and used the paper to roll cigarettes. The Bibles also fell victim to this.

There were views that they should have written more in the Bible in order to get more paper for their papyrus.

Everything in the way of paper was used, school books, newspapers. Machorka (Russian: Махорка) is a Russian tobacco variety made from the tobacco Nicotiana rustica (also known as farmer's tobacco), which was once grown by Native Americans in eastern North America and is now grown almost exclusively in Poland and Russia.

Machorka[28] is usually smoked as papirossa or as a self-rolled cigarette. It is unsuitable for use as pipe tobacco.

The farmer's tobacco is only coarsely cut; The nicotine content is very high, and imports into the EU are prohibited.

The Papirossa Machorka cigarette, which was previously widely used by Russian soldiers, now has a symbolic feature for the Soviet period of Russian history.

Among other things, German soldiers became familiar with tobacco in the war against the Soviet Union during World War II; in the jargon of the time, the Germans also called Machorka Stalin Hedge. In Soviet captivity, Machorka was sometimes distributed as part of the food allocations.

Even the family trees of families written down by themselves were burned as papyrus paper.

---

[28] More info and pictures are available at: https://sv.wikipedia.org/wiki/Bondtobak

A lot of valuable information disappeared in this way. You can read about this in *Quietly flows the Don* by Mikhail Sjolochov, a work of 5 volumes for which he received the Nobel Prize in Literature in 1965. He was a great friend of Sweden and spent some time in Sweden.

An interesting observation is that in the Soviet power the symbols of the hammer and sickle were used as an expression of the identity of the communist ideology.

The hammer in Russian becomes the molot and the sickle becomes the serp.

If you combine both these words (molotserp) and read the word backwards, you get the word (prestolom); with the throne.

Whether it is a tall tale or if there is any truth in it, I let the reader decide for himself.

A throne must of course have someone who sits and broods on it.

So perhaps the revolution and communism were aimed at removing the tsar from the throne and ascending it themselves. Or what was the purpose?

The Cossacks who participated in the counter-revolution did not want Jews in their ranks. What this may be due to is a question that only the Cossacks themselves can answer. Perhaps there was an averse general attitude towards this ethnic group for some reason.

Was the revolution staged to remove the Tsar and take power themselves with the help of the people under the pretext that it was a people's revolution but that the purpose was never to give anything to the people.

The real architects of this were a completely different group of people where there is a list of names of the rulers behind the vulnerable simple population and their blood that they sacrificed for something that actually had a completely different purpose from the beginning. The motives were obscure and insidious.

To officially go out and preach that the revolution was for the working people and in the form of a hammer as a representative of the industrial worker and the sickle as a representative of the hard-working peasant then becomes distasteful.

The only thing that reflects the true image will be the red colour of the flag as a representative of all the blood spilled by the simple population.

ESTONIA UNDER WWII

When my father and his comrades chose to go to war as young boys to defend their Estonia, they did so out of concern for their country. They could not do this in Estonian uniform, but had to put on a German uniform to fight against the Russian Bolsheviks.

When they ended up in refugee camps in Germany after the war, many of their compatriots who had fled Estonia distanced themselves from the young men who had gone to war to try to defend their/their country.

Feliks Virro (1926 - 1979)

Feliks Virro circa 1955

What Estonia's official position is today, regarding the young boys' participation in the defence of their country, is unclear to me.

The Germans occupied Estonia during July-August 1941 by Army Group North.

In the autumn of 1941, police battalions in the Baltic States were formed by volunteers on the initiative of the German authorities. According to German law, they were not allowed to be part of the Wehrmacht as they were not Germans. How was father counted when his grandmother was married to a German man?

These police battalions were initially intended to be used only in Baltic territory.

But in reality, they were used on the Eastern Front against partisans to exercise repression and guard duties.

The volunteers were often motivated by a desire for revenge[29] against the suffering they had been subjected to by the Soviet occupying power.

They were also deployed in Poland, Ukraine and Belarus. At the beginning of 1942, 12,000 Estonians, 20,000 Lithuanians and 14,000 Latvians fought on the German side against the Red Army.

In 1941, Germany did not allow larger national army units than at battalion level, but the more pressured the situation became with the fortunes of the war, the attitude changed, which led to the start of a recruitment of volunteers to national SS legions in 1942 - 1943.

But since not so many people took the plunge to join the voluntary offer, they mobilized instead.

In Estonia, this resulted in the establishment of the 20th Estonian SS Division. Correspondingly, 2 SS divisions were established in Latvia.

At the division level, these were led by Germans. From the regimental level, the command was Estonian and Latvian respectively.

The soldiers received the best available weapons training, which they later hoped to use in the interests of their own free nation.

At the beginning of 1944, a general mobilization of the occupying forces was declared and with this manpower 6 regiments were established which, together with the legions, fought to defend their national borders against the advancing Red Army.

Approximately 60,000 Estonians and over 100,000 Latvians fought with the German army in 1944.

---

[29] Similar ideas are present today in Estonia.

The 15th Latvian and 20th Estonian Divisions fought in 1945 on German territory and the 19th Latvian Division in Courland.

Most of the surviving soldiers were captured by the Red Army and some fled to the West, including my father.

There were also Estonians[30] and Latvians who fought for the Red Army.

This became evident at the end of the war, at the Battle of Narva, where Estonian soldiers in German and Russian uniforms faced each other on the battlefield and fought each other. They may have been neighbours in the same village.

Father probably joined as a volunteer (a little unclear when). He wanted to join the war to defend his fatherland against Bolshevism. It is important to understand that he and many other young Estonian men and boys did not join to fight on Hitler's side, but to fight against Bolshevism. Something that after the war was confirmed by the American forces, who let Estonian (also Latvian) former soldiers in the German army guard the Nazis during the Nuremberg trials. In the beginning, none of the young soldiers in Estonia knew how the war would develop with all the horrific abuses against the civilian population, which was done by both sides. Incidentally, there were also a considerable number of Jews who fought in the German army, a figure I have seen on Wikipedia gives about 150,000.

A piece of information I received from Estonia, see below

---

[30] August Kork among others

Feliks Virro, born in 14.3.1926 was Freiwillige, belonged to Estonian SS-Legion/Brigade/Division and had grade Grenadier, that's soldier. His first unit was Estnische Schutzmannschafts Abteilung 36 (later renamed Estnische Polizei Front Bataillon 36) with Politseipataljon, he fought in Stalingrad area.

(If he fought in Stalingrad, it must have been between August 1942 - February 1943, when the fighting in Stalingrad took place).

An acquaintance has dug into the history of Battalion Narwa and has managed to straighten out some questions about Father's time in the army – among other things, he has managed to locate a place where Father was wounded. The village, which is referred to by the Estonians in the battalion as Silov, was named Schiloff in German.

The Red Army launched several attacks on the village in early September (the hardest attack was on the 9th - 10th - day when father was wounded).

After being wounded on 10 September 1943 in Schiloff - it seems Feliks was back in Estonia in October.

It may have been on this occasion that Feliks had knocked on his mother's kitchen window and almost scared her out of her mind, as she was unaware that he was back in his home country, albeit temporarily.

On October 23, 1943, the soldiers from Wiking Narva were on leave in Estonia and celebrated the 2nd anniversary of the liberation of Estonia in the Narva City Theatre.

(The humorous performance "At the Dentist" provoked incessant bursts of laughter from the non-serving officer Wartenberg and the soldier Virro.) It seems to have been a funny performance. Feliks was as far as known the only soldier with the name Virro in this battalion (Narwa).

142

His commander in SS-Pz. Gren.Btl. "Narwa" 1. comp.was Captain Jaan Raudsoo.

Before the fighting at Schiloff, the group fought in Izum.

July 5, 1943 the German forces began an attack on the Arc of Kursk with one of the biggest tank battles of the Second World War. The strength used in this operation practically determined the whole destiny of the war. The military operation had two stages: in Kursk-Oryol area from July 5 until August 18, in Belgorod-Oryol area (the so-called Izium base) from July 17 until August 23. The German Army Group Mitte, led by Feldmarschall Hans Günther von Kluge (photo: on the left) and Army Group Süd, led by Feldmarschall Erich von Manstein (photo: on the right) were on one side. The Army Group Süd also included motorized Waffen-SS Division Wiking, under which Battalion Narva operated. On the other side were the Red Army's Brjansk, Southwest, Middle, Voronezh and Steppe front units.

Jaan Raudsoo was killed on the third day of the fighting at Izum.

Men in his company remember him as a caring and at the same time courageous officer. In the most difficult moment of the battle, he ran from one crater to the other — sleeves rolled up and the buttons of his soldier's coat open. He always had drinking water to share and even words of encouragement to his crew.

After the fighting at Izum, an evaluation was made of the outcome and it was concluded that although the German forces were to retreat, the Estonian soldiers did not. One can probably rightly attribute great courage to the Estonian soldiers in the situation they found themselves in.

The German army leaders had taken the Estonians retreat into account, but it seemed incredible for the Germans that it never actually happened. When the battle ended, the local headquarters made a report for the Army Group Süd's headquarters about what had happened. The leader of the Süd headquarters, being aware of the situation on the front, couldn't believe the report and sent its control commission on the spot. The commissions act was found from the archive by German veterans and it said: There were 650 Estonian men in Izium battles, they had 3 German and 2 Soviet anti-tank cannons, magnetic mines and plenty of heavy machine guns MG-34 and MG-42, in addition they had submachine guns. The Russian side had more than 20,000 attackers and more than 100 tanks supported them. Like it was stated in the Middle Front's control commission's act, more than 9,000 attacker's bodies were left on the battlefield and 113 tanks were destroyed. Estonians lost 69 men and 6 Germans, the next battle had a little more than 250 men, the others were hospitalised, most of them with mild injuries.

A brief overview of father's involvement during the war could be as follows:

36th Police Battalion at Stalingrad, transfer to the Estonian Legion, training in Germany, service in the 1st Infantry Division. company/SS Panzer Grenadier Battalion "Narwa", wounded at Schiloff 10/9 1943, hospital, then back to Estonia - probably at Füsilier Battalion 20 (formerly Battalion Narwa), again wounded, hospital, and last a minimum deployment in Silesia in any of the division's units.

At the Battle of Rostov on July 23, 1942, armoured personnel from the SS Wiking Division participated, backing up the 13th and 22nd Panzer Divisions for an assault right into the heart of Rostov all the way to the main bridge over the Don River. The fighting was violent, especially against the troops defending the NKVD headquarters, but at the end of the following day the last pockets of defence were shattered in a systematic cleansing, building by building. It is unclear whether father was present at Rostov.

This battalion (36. The Police Battalion) was also involved in fighting in Novogrudek, Belarus on August 7, 1942. There are reports of questionable efforts by the battalion. I don't know if my father was involved in this.

Father may have been there; he was reportedly present at Stalingrad and this battle preceded the attack on Stalingrad. They were in Stalingrad between November 22 and December 31, 1942.

There was an Elmar Vilumäe who was the commander (lieutenant) of the 2nd group, the 3rd company of the 36th Police Battalion, a battalion consisting of 600 men. If it is as I think that Elmar Vilumäe is the same person as Elmar Viitismann-Vilumäe, then probably my father was in the same company. Elmar and father visited his father's cousin Gerda in Hamm in 1943. Gerda remembers Elmar as she thought he was very handsome. Father also has a photo of a Lembit and it could be Lembit Vaher. He was (lieutenant) in the 2nd rifle company.

An important part of the Russian soldiers' acquisition was the allocation of liquor they received every day, 100 grams. When there was no liquor, they resorted to industrial spirits and also antifreeze agents intended for their engines, which they purified through the activated carbon contained in their gas masks. Many soldiers had thrown away their gas masks from the previous year, so the activated carbon in the remaining gas masks became hard currency to be able to purify this antifreeze. Unfortunately, many became ill or blind from this and some died, which was also the case for my father, even though it was in Sweden and more than 30 years later. The stresses during the war were severe and the alcohol helped to keep the anxiety at bay. Therefore, they were able to resort to the drastic method of trying to purify unfit alcohol into drinkable alcohol. To be able to maintain their oral hygiene somewhat, they used a finger as a toothbrush that they put a little salt on. Even during the Korean War, it could be seen that alcohol was a way to numb anxiety. At least if you have seen the TV series M.A.S.H about American doctors who in primitive forms patch up American and Korean soldiers and sometimes even Chinese (War is hell).

The Russians and Germans had two different methods of knocking out each other's tanks. The Germans lay in trenches waiting for the Russians' tanks to pass over the trench and they were then quick to attach a magnetic mine under the tanks. The Russians had a more sophisticated method; they used dogs they had trained through Pavlov's classical conditioning to carry an explosive charge attached to their backs and run under the tank where they were later detonated with a remote-controlled control of the Russians or the antenna attached to the backs of the dogs. When the dogs got under the tank, the antenna hit the chassis, which caused the mine to explode. The dogs had been trained to ensure that there was food under the tanks[31].

In October 1942, an Estonian SS legion was formed. This fought during 1943 - 1944 as the SS Panzar Grenadier Battalion "Narwa" in Ukraine. It was then at a place called Schiloff, where father was wounded for the first time, in his right little finger. Schiloff was located in eastern Ukraine, southwest of Dobropolje.

---

[31] Later research has shown that the Russian dogs ran under their own tanks that they had trained on.

At the beginning of 1944, the Estonian brigade was expanded into one division. In February 1944, the 20th Grenadier Division Waffen SS was subordinated to the Narva front under III. SS-Panzer Corps.

In June 1944, my father was wounded in the fighting by shrapnel in his throat and was admitted to a hospital in Riga from where, after about two months of care and in connection with the evacuation of Estonia by the German troops, he was transferred to Danzig, where he was admitted to a German hospital.

From there he was transferred to Magdeburg and discharged in the autumn of 1944. After 4 months of further training as a non-commissioned officer, he was transferred to an Estonian unit and then participated in the fighting on the Eastern Front until the beginning of May 1945.

There are gaps in what I know about his experiences, but assumptions supported by fragments of conversations he uttered while growing up were that he had seen his friends get hanged in Czechoslovakia. There is one event that can prove this; On 5 - 8 May 1945, at the very end of the war, he had been in Czechoslovakia in an Estonian regiment, the 20th SS Division. They were guarding a radio station in Prague that the Germans had control of when they were attacked by Czech partisans. The Czechs took over the station and the Estonians surrendered in return for the promise of free passage, which was not kept by the partisans, they chased down the Estonian soldiers who had surrendered and surrendered their weapons only to be betrayed in their promises. Full panic broke out and the Germans had to flee head over heels out of the city in all they could get their hands on when it came to vehicles. The partisans went around with Estonian prisoners on truck beds and hung them from lampposts and other hangers.

More than 500 Estonian soldiers were killed or wounded during these gauntlets. My father and his friends managed to break out of this hell, a hell that has been described as "The Czech Hell" in the history description of the event (can be read about on Wikipedia). They had given up the war, but the hatred from the Czechs was so strong that this event could play out so dramatically. The incident was so traumatic that one of the friends that my father came with to Sweden never got a driver's license. He remembered the escape through the streets of Prague in the vehicle they had at their disposal, and what exactly took place during the journey can only be speculated about. Perhaps the partisans stood in the way of the fleeing Germans, who did not shy away in their panic from escaping the partisans to whom they had capitulated, but who thus betrayed their promises.

Examples of broken promises

The escape went west, where they were captured or surrendered to the American troops.

According to the United States, the day and place of his capture were not recorded until before September 3 to 9, 1946, and he was released from captivity on October 8, 1946.

He was also part of an American guard force that guarded the Nazis during the Nuremberg Trials after WWII.

The company's name was 4221 and there was also a Latvian equivalent guard company.

US Army, Estonian Guard Company 4221 or 4221 Labor Service Company.

They were all former Waffen SS soldiers and they served as prison guards for war criminals at the Nuremberg trials. The United States trusted them because they were not Nazis but were considered freedom fighters. Many of these men later went to the United States and served in the U.S. Army (Korea, Vietnam, etc.—mostly as instructors—they had received solid military training in the SS).

Father had also been in London in August 1947 and received an Estonian temporary passport before taking the boat to Sweden.

In September the same year he went to Kiel with the intention of fleeing to Sweden. In the port of Kiel, he and three other Estonians sneaked aboard a Swedish ship, where they hid in the coal cargo.

How was my grandmother's life affected after the war by my father's participation on the German side of the war? I have seen information that they could have a hard time, the relatives. Could it have influenced my aunt Endla's deportation to Vorkuta that my father had been in the war? What did the Russians know about my father's time in the German army? Did Grandma get intrusive questions from the Russians?

Every year, Waffen-SS veterans of the 20th SS detachment of WWII hold rallies and celebrate their fight against the Red Army. They call themselves Estonia's freedom fighters. The number of members in the club is 3,000 I have seen on a website. The number is decreasing every year as more people drop out due to old age and the ranks are thinning out. How does Estonia officially view these freedom fighters today? It was for their country that they fought their battles.

Feliks´ first time in Sweden

Information he himself gave to the Swedish authorities when he came to Sweden in September 1947 is that he was born on 14 March 1926 in Tartu, Estonia, within the marriage of Estonian citizens, the now deceased butcher Jan Virro and his surviving wife Maria, née Arola (Arula), married and that he (Feliks) was registered and lives in Norrköping, St. Johannes's parish, at Vrinnevigatan 19, and employed as a rubber worker by the rubber factory company Goodyear. He was brought up in his parents' home and attended elementary school for six years and two years for secondary school. He was confirmed in the Evangelical Lutheran doctrine. After finishing school in 1943, he took a permanent position in the Estonian army and then, after training in the infantry, participated in the battles against the Russians.

I understand that Father did not want to talk about all this in Sweden, because "The only foreign powers to recognize the Soviet annexation of Estonia in 1940 were Nazi Germany and Sweden".

More than 300 000 citizens of Estonia - almost a third of its population at the time - were affected by mass arrests, mass murders, deportations and other acts of repression. As a result of the communist occupation,

150

Estonia permanently lost at least 200,000 people or 20% of its population to oppression, emigration and war.

What I can't understand is why he stated that his mother's name as unmarried was Arola when it was Wirro. My grandmother had a sister (half-sister) named Arula who was married. He has also stated in Germany that his mother's name was Arula.

On December 12, 1958, my father was granted Swedish citizenship and with this decision, my sister and I were also granted the same, mother became a Swedish citizen in 1947. The application process included an investigation into the "foreigner's" conduct in which the employer and the housing provider were allowed to submit a statement on the person's conduct. I don't know if this is still applied in Sweden to obtain Swedish citizenship? It was Detective Constable Erik Pålsson at the Crime Department in Norrköping who carried out this investigation and he obtained information that nothing was to blame him. It was nothing but praise. In the report, you can read that all employers and landlords had submitted information, a fairly thorough review. A parking offence in 1956 was also noted where father was fined SEK 20. He also had to certify that there had been no mental or other serious illness in his family and that he feels fully healthy and able to work. The shape of the face and the anatomy of the nose were also described in the investigation, in this case oval face shape and straight nose. My mother's face shape was also oval but the nose concave.

Before father came to Norrköping, he came to Stockholm as a stowaway on a boat from Kiel together with 3 comrades. They had illegally sneaked onto a boat in Kiel without the crew's knowledge. They arrived in Stockholm on 22 September 1947 and were granted an alien's

151

passport (7590/47) valid until 1 June 1948, as well as a residence permit (K.2628) for residence in Finspång's county fiscal district, Östergötland County, for the period 2 December 1947 – 1 March 1948. They had read through an advertisement in Swedish newspapers in Stockholm that there was work to be had at Ängenäs. This was the reason why they travelled to Finspång. They were offered work as forest workers at Ängenäs, Ysunda, in Finspång town. There were several Estonians who found work as forestry workers there. On Saturdays they took the boat and rowed across the lake Glan to get into Norrköping and party and on one occasion a boat capsized and a man named Elmar Hio drowned on October 3, 1947.

When they first came to Ängenäs, they were dressed in their suits and were allowed to buy work clothes when they were paid.

Father moved to Norrköping on 29 February 1948 where he rented a room on the travelling floor Garvaregatan 44 until 7 April 1948. Between 7 April 1948 and 15 April 1950, he lived at Strandvägen 4 - 6, Norrköping, with his landlady Anna Andersson. He spent a couple of short periods at sea during this time, but then had this residence as a base.

Between 16 April 1950 and 21 May 1953, my father rented a home in Högalund's garden from the gardener David Andersson. He had then married my mother Flora on 22 April 1950 in Ö-Eneby parish in Norrköping. That same year, my sister was born on July 6th. The marriage certificate states the father as a Soviet Russian citizen and the mother as a Swedish citizen.

On 22 May 1953, the family moved to a rented apartment at Trädgårdsgatan 36, Norrköping, a property owned by H.S.B.

From there the family moved on 1 May 1955 to Västra S:t Persgatan 35, Norrköping.

From Västra S:t Persgatan 35 we moved to Vrinnevigatan 19 on February 1, 1958, which was then a new area. Mother lived there until 2010 when she died. I think it coincided with my father getting a residence permit. The situation was very unclear before he got the residence permit. What would have happened otherwise? Could my restlessness have its bottom from this time? It must have affected the whole family's life. Mother's siblings and families had Swedish citizenship since 1947, while we were waiting to get it. There are many families today who live in this insecurity and it becomes easier to understand what they are suffering. There was no such thing as SFI (Swedish for Immigrants) but it went well anyway because they were sent out directly into society and got to work and thus, they learned Swedish and the culture they were welcomed into.

Flora Virro (Adelman) 1929 – 2010)

Flora Virro in her 50s

The name Adelman, which is my mother's maiden name, is a very old name. Whether it can be shown whether my branch of the name can be traced back to the first mentions of the name, I cannot ascertain from the documents I have seen, but it is a tantalizing thought.

154

I have found another branch of the name Adelmann in the Tartu area. This branch has branches down to Germany while my branch is said to have been named Adelman in 1835 or close to it. However, I have not seen any evidence that this is the case. Apparently, there is both a German and a Jewish branch of the name. The spelling of the name also varies, sometimes with an n at the end and sometimes with two. It's something you find in many names, different spellings. The name was written down more as it sounded, sometimes it could be difficult to read also what was written in the church books. It is different today when computers can receive any characters.

Whether the name Adelman was assigned by the local baron or if the name has been in the family for a long time is difficult to determine, but if you consider that a baron could assign his peasants any name they wanted, one can wonder why the family got such a grand name in this context? It was just a matter of thanking and bowing for the name you were given.

Considering that my ancestors on my mother's side have Estonian-Swedish roots, it will be an exciting thought if this name has wandered through all of Europe from southwestern Germany up through Germany to Sweden and then on to the western parts of Estonia. When the family fled from Estonia to Sweden, was it to flee home or has there been another "home" for the family before Estonia as well?

The farm that mother grew up on and had to leave was called Asundus Vidriku and was 29 hectares in size. The farm was located on Nuckö or Noarootsi, which is the Estonian name. Nuckö is located in western Estonia near Haapsalu, a small coastal town. The area has been Swedish-linked for perhaps as much as 1000 years. Grandpa spoke Swedish at home as a child according to a statement I have.

Research by Jonathan Lindström claims that there was a forced emigration from Öland to the islands off Estonia in the 13th century.

The Germans who were stationed on Nuckö in 1944 were aware that grandfather was building a boat. They used to come by. They realized that the Russians would soon occupy Estonia again and were probably just waiting to be evacuated from there, the war was lost.

My mother and her family left Nuckö, Estonia at the end of June/July 1944.

Mother came with her family to Sweden via Åland and Finland in a boat that some of the men had built. The engine they had installed in the boat was an ignition ball engine that had been in a combine. One of the men who lived in Haapsalu could read nautical charts and was allowed to accompany him. On the trip there was also a lot of home-brewed beer that even the appointed navigator drank with the result that they got off course. A Finnish reconnaissance aircraft noticed their situation and contacted the Finnish Coast Guard, who came to their rescue and towed the boat to Mariehamn on Åland.

There they got to take a sauna, eat and rest before the trip continued to Turku in Finland on a much larger and safer boat. The boat that the trip was made with from Estonia remained in Åland, as well as the beer keg and also my uncle Einar's new boots. So, Einar had to go from Mariehamn to Turku without boots. However, he was given new boots when he arrived in Turku, where they then had to wait a few days until the consul had arranged an entry visa to Sweden.

From Turku, the journey continued by liner boat to Stockholm, where they were placed at Sabbatsberg Hospital, where they stayed for a week and where they were also vaccinated against tuberculosis. Then the journey continued to Doverstorp outside Finspång, a refugee camp that included 200 refugees. They got a change of clothes there. As my grandfather was a farmer, the family was placed at Rönö Kungsgård in Vikbolandet. Grandfather worked, among other things, with ditching for the farmer. Einar, who was 14 years old, had to drive materials forward by horse and cart. Mother was 15 years old and had to work as a maid on the farm.

Einar's salary was 25 öre per hour and his mother's salary was 1 krona a day. Mother's two sisters stayed at Grandma's house. The youngest son Alvar was not born then.

They stayed at Rönö Kungsgård in Vikbolandet over the winter of 1944/1945.

After this, they moved into Norrköping, to a place called "Blåsut. There were two apartments on the upper floor, a slightly larger one-room apartment and a smaller one-room apartment. In the slightly larger one lived grandfather's sister with her family. There were 4 people who lived there plus my mother and Einar.

In the smaller one lived grandfather and grandmother with Hilma and Sara plus Alvar who was born there on December 10, 1946.

My grandmother worked as a seamstress until my grandfather got a job at YFA as a dyer of woollen yarns.

My grandfather worked there until his retirement. He died of cancer on April 23, 1974.

Grandma sewed clothes at home for friends and acquaintances for a small fee. She also sewed clothes for the family, I remember, among other things she sewed trousers for me.

When grandfather's sister and family moved out of their slightly larger one-room apartment, both apartments became available to grandfather and family. It was completely outdated apartments with a water pump a good distance from the house. The outhouse was also a good distance from the house where the slush bucket was also emptied.

ESTONIA OF TODAY

As a member of the EU and NATO, Estonia has today, together with most of the countries in the EU, taken a very stubborn anti-Russian stance with an army of 7,000 soldiers of its own. It seems like a small overdue task to show such teeth to the Russian bear. Without taking a political stand for or against Russia, one should perhaps calm down a little and once again resort to what used to be called diplomacy, but which unfortunately today has been replaced by a blind, hateful war-mongering. I suppose the official position today in Estonia would be that the young boys and even girls who are prepared to attack Russia should be celebrated.

TROUBLED TIMES IN EUROPE TODAY

What seems to be happening today is that many people in Europe are tired of the decadence and hypocrisy that is spreading thru Europe. Just look at the big headlines what the Reichsbürger movement in Germany has created, which seems to be the beginning of an awakening in Europe that sees a clear annihilation of the former population and its existence.

There is a great deal of concern about what the countries of Europe see as a future. What is called a threat to democracy is perhaps in fact a cry for democracy. All the decisions that are made today by EU bureaucrats where the ordinary person is forgotten are in fact an organization of gigantic proportions where the biggest fiddlers gather around the honey jar. Where there is money, there are always criminals and other suspect, shady elements who, in their own interpretation of democracy, profit at the expense of others.

If you trumpet your own interpretation of democracy often enough, it sticks in people's minds as a true interpretation. But it is important to get an arena where you can shout out your message, right or wrong.

There are documents that relate to the Russian Revolution of 1917 and the involvement of the Jewish people. A document in Russian naming a number of high representatives of the positions after the revolution were Jewish, Prince Reuss points to this and also Hans von Rosen who lost everything, he as well as the rest of the nobility. Why does the Jewish population always appear in these contexts?

How to know if a document is genuine is a question that you should always ask yourself and it becomes more difficult every year to decide.

Is there any connection to what Hans von Rosen writes about here in 1926? Were the tendencies clear even then? These are the concluding words that Hans wrote:

.........In accordance with tradition, members of the former noble Congress were elected to the Council of the General Society. Having previously been Deputy Land Marshall, I had been given the presidency which I still hold. I consider it my task to take care of and keep alive the ancient spirit of Vidzemes' chivalry, in close cooperation with the Verband des Livländischen Stammadels, which unites representatives of the nobility in Germany and which I regularly attend in Berlin. At our last meeting in May of this year, which was attended by 230 representatives of chivalry, it gave us great hope and confirmed our spiritual strength.

May it survive all the storms of the future!

Lielstraupe, august 1926

Baron Hans Rosen

After the introductory words about how the structure of the different societies was and the human condition has been examined a bit, the question arises whether it was better in the past and whether it is possible to see from this why societies today look the way they do.

Were there indications even then of what is happening now, that everything has been a long journey of events that are connected.

I am prepared to say that this is the case as I have examined my own background with difficulties that have existed and still exist and based on my observations that are extremely limited to those in my family tree and people in the social sphere around them, have given that it is possible to explain certain situations about how the people have acted.

A person's choices in life are not only an ill-considered action, but are also based on past experiences and experiences.

Sometimes everything can change within just a couple of years. The structure that had been built up in Prussia for a long time was snatched away with great drama in just a few years.

Of course, one can ask oneself the question of the legitimacy and fairness of the system and also ask whether it has improved. The gradual slide from communism to democracy and on to liberalism is inevitably heading towards anarchy, where we are unfortunately already in some respects with widespread greed in all parts of society.

Perhaps it needs to go to the point where society collapses fully before a reconstruction can take over and the whole cycle repeats itself?

As previously described, as early as December 1825, a group of Russian aristocrats and military personnel started an uprising demanding reform. The revolt was put down and many of the rebels were deported to Siberia, where some became farmers and landowners, while others started schools. Others were not as fortunate. Landowners could expel healthy, young male farmers, often with their families to settle in the area. Most of those who were deported to Siberia lived a hard life in crushing poverty.

At the same time, the country experienced several peasant revolts and persecution of intellectuals. Tsar Nicholas I did not pursue his father's more liberal policies and made it almost impossible for people from the lower classes to obtain higher education.

Russian peasants who were stuck in their serfdom ran away from their masters and were called Cossacks and settled in the area around the Don River. They were good horse people.

And Quiet Flows the Don (Tichij Don) by Mikhail Sjolochov was an interesting book to read. It was at home on my bookshelf when I grew up but it was in Estonian so I couldn't read it until much later in life in Swedish.

The Swedish philosopher Lars Adelskogh has emphasized:

The ignorance of the people is the strength of the rulers.

Amen to this.

LIFE TODAY IN SWEDEN

When diversity is a watchword in Sweden today, it can be perceived that if you advocate this, it can have some unexpected consequences. I myself have a small flower bed on my patio where I have a number of flowers that I have tried to keep track of. It was the previous apartment owner who had planted an infinite number of bulbs that she kept after in an exemplary way.

But when I now try to do the same thing after a few years, it doesn't go as well. It's starting to look wild and I've had a bit of a bad conscience about it. I have a hard time working in the soil with my arms because of my back and it grows a bit as it wants now.

But it struck me the other day that this is how it should be, we embrace a wild diversity system which should also include our flower beds. It can be perceived as an excuse, and it is to some extent, but a slightly deeper meaning is that it becomes visible what diversity is.

Some think it looks good while others think it looks terrible. But if you appreciate the diversity of the Swedish population, you probably appreciate a slightly wild flower bed as some would see it while others then see this beautiful diversity. Everything that grows is beautiful?

The question is whether this is good or bad? Seeing how diversity changes a flower bed with a variety of new species, new species may be offensive to some, but our politicians would certainly appreciate this

162

flowerbed. I need to keep an eye on my flower bed now for invasive species that can take over the entire bed without me being aware of it.

Even though my search is over for this time, the questions have not become fewer, but rather the opposite, but I have learned a lot and need to acquire greater knowledge to be able to interpret and evaluate my material.

Some parts I have been able to get answers to while other parts have just given me more questions.

It was a journey about what the countries that influenced my ancestors looked like and the changes that have taken place. The geography lesson I have received has also meant lessons about politics and history. Even concepts such as PTSD and Epigenetics have been circulating in my head. How did all this really fit together? Does it need to be connected or is it just life that goes on its own way. It has also started up a lot of new thoughts that I otherwise wouldn't have had, some scary and dark for me.

As my trip showed, nothing was only black or white, but it was very much in grey scales and also filled with colourful shades.

There has been a lot of digging into and analysing the material I have found with the help of the internet and information from archives, genealogy sites and other institutions.

Thoughts about life and its different phases have also been generated and how politically questionable decisions and values have influenced my own thoughts in a sometimes frightening and for me a completely new direction. Why these thoughts appeared is a question I have asked myself countless times during the process, but if everything were fine in a society, these thoughts would not have to arise?

Perhaps one should ask oneself why so many thoughts about conspiracy arise in society and who actually has the right ideas. If you are going to be critical in your thinking, you have to be so against the prevailing narrative as well, otherwise you have made the mistake of not being critical of sources and then the whole narrative collapses like a castle in the air.

When asked if it was better in the past, it is not easy to compare different time periods, but the picture that emerges and that has been analysed after 50 - 80 years becomes the prevailing true picture and one asks, again, how could it be like that. Walking around in the middle of chaos means that you cannot see the whole picture of social development. A number of years ago it was fashionable to get a helicopter view, you had to see everything a little from above to get some perspective and distance. Perhaps the helicopter has been retired and no new one is available.

To just follow the broad masses and adopt its broad narrative may now seem simple and reasonable, but in 50 - 80 years' time you may ask the question again, why did no one react to this. The issue is also relevant in today's societies. I am also thinking of the situation in Germany in the 1930s/1940s, how could it arise and why did not more people oppose the development.

Airing my thoughts and getting them on paper has been an eye-opener for me.

I have had to re-evaluate old thoughts and values and gained new approaches to my thinking on certain questions, questions that have seemed easy to answer but which then turned out to be not so easy to answer.

THE PARADISE OF THE SINECURES

Living in a society where many strive to obtain a sinecure and just want an income without contributing to society seems to be becoming more common every year and something that is creeping down the ages from previously having been granted to decrepit politicians and fired directors general. Can you not see income support as something that also falls under this concept? No quid pro quo is required. August Strindberg was the first person as far as I know to receive a sinecure at a library in Stockholm, but that was a number of years ago?

Since I am no longer available to the labour market and thus do not visit the Public Employment Service, I wonder if there is a special code for applying for sinecures? A rather vague description of what these services entail should suffice, even without content with only a statement about who conveys the salary envelope. Perhaps there will be a shift towards sinecures for most positions, the requirements to perform a job will disappear with reference to the fact that it can be perceived as offensive and downright racist to have to perform a quid pro quo for one's salary. Offering an employer to pay a salary to a sinecurist is a great favour for the employer and should render the employer to solemnly bow to the sinecurist and ask if he is satisfied with the content, otherwise an adjustment is made until the sinecurist is satisfied. A salary is a fundamental right that should not have to be linked to a performance with a knowledge behind it, AI can do that. Society must find someone who wants to voluntarily undertake to perform the tasks that AI cannot handle.

THOUGHTS IN THE PRESENT

In Sweden and a number of other countries, we have something the politicians call democracy. The more I think about what it is, the more lost I get in my thoughts and the more unclear the concept appears. Is it a concept that you use to package an approach to your surroundings or is it a shadow that you hide behind in order to be able to usurp resources from society that you are not really entitled to or otherwise qualified for? If you are ignorant in general, it can be good to throw yourself around with the concept of democracy, then society opens up like an institution where even unqualified individuals demand a right they are not really entitled to.

The most important thing is to be kind to these people. Are you allowed to call them people at all or is it seen as racist? It is difficult today to know what can and cannot be said, someone will probably be offended anyway.

But it is important that those who scream the loudest get their way, they have probably suffered the most of all in life and should be compensated. But if a doctor arrives at the scene of an accident with a number of injured people, the doctor is likely to focus on the person who cannot scream and who is in a more serious situation than the person who can scream and gape.

To emphasize one's own suffering, one can attack someone else and thus shift the focus from one's own deed, thus distancing oneself from responsibility.

Our wise politicians are happy to participate in various gimmicks and thus hope to win some political points. If you can also discredit your political opponents and their voters, then happiness is complete and the politicians go into a spin and this is then praised by our established media as a very important step for the country, or especially for democracy.

If you mention the word democracy, you have surrounded yourself with a padded cocoon as protection against criticism and you sit calmly and safely in there and cuddle and know that you are unassailable in all your self-righteousness. One can then go out into the streets and squares without blinking or reflecting on one's own actions and shout and attack one's fellow human beings with violence without feeling remorse.

Self-awareness is unfortunately something that can be difficult. That the right hand should need to know what the left hand is doing can be difficult to achieve.

A bistro is considered by many today to be a refined concept that you like to throw around without knowing where the word comes from. The word is used because it is considered a little finer.

But the word bistro comes from the Russian word for fast (быстро).

When Napoleon had attacked Russia in the early 1800s and then been chased back to France, the Russian soldiers were hungry and wanted food quickly, so they shouted быстро when they wanted to be served without delay.

It is a little strange that this expression has not been included on the list of sanctions against Russia when it is now urgent to show decisiveness. Maybe even politicians visit a bistro sometimes?

It was a small parenthesis just considering how you throw around concepts without understanding the meaning or background, maybe it's the same with the word democracy.

To simply hide behind the word democracy, much like it would include everything from being moral, honest, kind-hearted and generally cuddly. It has gained a strength this word, completely in the class of the word racist. Just mentioning the word racist makes the other party silent so as not to risk being tainted and accused of being a racist. But a person who in this situation accuses someone else of being a racist is in fact the one who is a racist. It is in that person's thoughts that the term occurs. If you want to question what the magic word means in a society, then you are accused of being anti-democratic. Being able to hold general elections is something you emphasize where all people can and can express their opinion however they want. How is this different from a country that does not adhere to democratic values?

If we take the United States as an example, that country is presented as the ultimate democracy in the world. In a democracy, you don't have the death penalty, but the United States does. The United States does not have free health care for everyone, but even though it applies the death penalty and does not have free health care, is it a democracy?

Is it the case that in the United States, when you are going to execute someone, you do it in a particularly American humane way, with the right values? Why is this not brought up more in the debate about the hypocrisy of the United States. Somehow it seems to be accepted that the United States is allowed to execute people within the framework of democracy, they are so amazing anyway. Can you then not establish the death penalty in Sweden as well, we could do it since we have the right values and are a pink superpower with a rainbow flag as a national symbol soon. If you feel that there is something wrong in a society and cannot express this without being suspected and being called a racist or other epithet that can be spat on by the large broad masses, at least officially, how should you express your concern?

It would be very serious if there were far more people who see the mismanagement of the country's economy that is going on but do not dare or have the energy to protest against it and join the large ignorant masses. Perhaps there is reason for the expression that - *If you can't beat them, join them.* Perhaps there is a crumb one can hope will fall from the politicians' table.

It hurts less then and then you hope that some other person or group will have the strength and courage to try to make things right and then you can feel a satisfaction in this. Then the concept of hypocrisy comes to mind again. The great underlying fear that many people feel deep down has devastating consequences for a country in crisis. If a country's political elite can spread this fear, it has a firm grip on its population. Unfortunately, it is probably the case that the one who screams the loudest about these concepts is the one who has the most to gain from the words not being dissected and what they really mean. In order for a democracy to function, hopefully certain conditions must be met in terms of mutual understanding and management of society's collective resources.

It is both responsibility and rights, but when democracy begins to be interpreted and eroded on the basis that you should only have rights in society, well, that's when things start to go wrong. But in practice, this means that no one decides as the fear of saying something wrong overshadows the action and the desired decision. An individual's (in)ability to be able to adhere to both of these principles in terms of responsibility and rights is something fundamental for society to be able to function.

Unfortunately, some people only focus on their rights as something that is taken for granted, while others realize that they have obligations too, perhaps mostly obligations.

Taking responsibility for one's actions and not taking everything for granted is something that is self-evident to many. But it seems that democracy in Sweden means that no one really takes responsibility, you rely on someone else to take care of a possible problem, or challenge as you insist on calling it. Problems don't seem to exist anymore in society, it sounds so nasty and cruel and someone can be singled out for something and it's very scary. In order to be able to talk about a challenge, there must be some underlying problem, sorry, challenge that is the challenge itself. Or do you ignore the underlying problem and how can you then find a solution if you don't know what the problem is? What is meant by challenge in the public debate? Have you mixed apples and pears a little wildly just to throw yourself with fluffy concepts?

It cannot be the case that one group just takes care of the rights and leaves the obligations to another group in society. It arises when an imbalance arises and groups begin to look at each other with suspicion and society begins to be pulled apart.

Some use the concept of democracy as a tool to only be able to steal with a clear conscience. How would these groups have managed to survive in an older society with completely different demands on citizens. Is it developing for a society that you allow everything; you even celebrate strongly deviant behaviours. Being a feminist is something great in today's society, something that our politicians proudly trumpet on the world's arenas that they are.

Today it is almost seen as a weakness to be so-called normal and must be fought at all costs, that you are almost a criminal. Defining normal is controversial, but as an individual you should be able to have the right to do it for yourself. Especially when you are not a public figure who is supposed to embrace everything and nothing.

170

Democracy roughly means popular government or people's power. A basic idea of democracy is that the vast majority of people who are citizens or live in a country should have the opportunity to participate and have their say on how the country should be governed, for example through regular elections.

Another basic democratic idea is that all people are of equal value and should have the same rights. In a democracy, you should be able to think and think what you want, as long as you follow the current narrative and then as a good citizen have the opportunity to express your opinions openly in speech or writing within the current narrative.

DEATH

What is death? A new stage that one achieves or an endless rest without hope? Why are most people so afraid of death? Are you conscious there and do you suffer in the same way as when you lived on earth. The Bible has written a lot about this. Are you tormented by someone or something for your previous (mis)deeds? Do you as a former human being have any consciousness at all then? You become a disembodied unit consisting of energies that are held together by, well, what? Magnetic fields or other physical or perhaps spiritual non-physical energies? If you start thinking about these things, you may begin to approach your own approaching experience of death and what it might mean to be dead.

Do you need to feel fear or can you with your head held high trudge straight into the jaws of death and face it with pride and anticipation? When you walk in the corridors of death and see the various doors open and where people disappear in at dizzying speed so you don't have time to see a glimpse of what it looks like on the other side, well, then you are close to being pulled in yourself. Curiosity has always been man's best friend and enemy. It has driven man to great deeds but also to horrific deeds.

It can cause unfortunate situations and consequences that can be difficult to foresee. All that remains after a life are memories of someone, memories that are fading away more and more. Imagine that we end up as memories only for some and for others nothing. For some, it can be good memories and for others bad memories. For the main character, it doesn't really matter much, or how should you look at it? Do good memories determine that you will be better off in life after death before a possible new start on earth? The soul that is said to live on gets better conditions in the next body. When one is born, it should be inculcated in the individual that it is important to acquire good memories and perform actions that are repaid with good memories in the aftermath. Nothing perishes, it just transforms.

DECEIT

A question that has followed me in recent years is whether Estonia, as a re-independent republic, has betrayed the young men and boys who during WWII gave their lives for the then occupied Estonia (the same applies to the other Baltic states).

They set out to try to drive the Russians out of their territory and the only way they could do it was in German uniforms.

Many of these soldiers had many traumatic memories from the war, and this applies to those who survived. My father was one of those who came to Sweden after the war and started a family here. As a little boy, I didn't know about anything else, only that my father didn't talk about his experiences other than a few fragments sometimes. How damaged

172

was he really by his experiences during the war? At that time, the concept of PTSD – Post-Traumatic Stress Disorder – did not exist and there was no talk at all about what had been. But the secrecy that surrounded my father affected me more than I realized at the time. It characterized my future life by not being seen so as not to draw attention to me in the same way as probably my father did. His seclusion made me think a lot, but I thought that everyone felt the same way as I did.

Is it that at the end of my life, I try to relate to the fact that I have suffered from PTSD? Can PTSD be passed on to a child? The events that I have been through and the greatest trauma when I became a father at a young age, plus my upbringing as a child, could it have triggered PTSD? Or was it a manifestation of PTSD? Has it meant that I have created an image of myself that is not really me? All my life I have acted based on what I have thought you should do in a certain situation. The question then becomes how to explain that I ran away from the responsibility of my eldest son? My actions do not coincide with how I have otherwise acted, in many cases I have acted pragmatically and in some cases out of fear. The action has been based on what others have expected of me or what has been required in the moment, much like a chameleon that adapts to its surroundings all the time but in the end does not know what the original colour looked like.

One explanation that has struck me recently is that I didn't feel like I could give a child what the child needed. I had no job or education, so the best thing for the child must be that the mother meets another man who has the prerequisites to give the child a decent life. I don't think I'll ever be able to answer why that happened. Was it just life itself that turned out like that?

Can betrayal be inherited and passed on? My grandmother's mother betrayed her daughter, my grandmother was abandoned and completely abandoned to a life on the fringes of society. My father was also betrayed by his father and my father betrayed me. In addition, I have betrayed my oldest son and how is my relationship with my other two sons, have I betrayed them too? I don't think so, even though I've always been able to do more, maybe. It is difficult to get an answer to such a question.

When the thoughts are buzzing in my head like a bunch of angry bees that have been frightened and no solution is visible, then I wish there was someone close to me who could explain and tread out the cobwebs into a manageable reality. Why do I punish myself with these constantly negative thoughts. Is it penance I seek in this way. I even consciously try to bring my thoughts even deeper into the swamp but I don't seem to get any further at the moment. What can I do to get away from these destructive and paralyzing thoughts? What do I hope to find when I get down to the bottom, what can be there besides the devil. Or is it a desire to get to the bottom and then find the way up.

MAKING MISTAKES RIGHT

Perhaps this is what politicians are doing to push through, or avoid acting by holding on to their positions, which then makes it easier for them to deceive their voters. Or they themselves believe in their arguments, right or wrong.

Deciding for yourself which premises you want to use to drive a logical conclusion as a basis for decisions is what all experts do. This becomes clear when two experts argue their case as correct in a conversation on TV, while the opponent is wrong. But if both are experts, who is

174

right? If you are an expert, you assume that that person has a little extra knowledge about the subject in question. But isn't it then just that they choose different premises from which they then draw conclusions with high confidence. What is an expert? It seems more like it's just a way to belittle your opponents and explain away their arguments. The little person will humbly bow before the authorities? You want to show some kind of strength by calling yourself an expert. It becomes a bit tragicomic.

Having a point of view may be more important than appearing human by saying they don't know the answer.

One way to give yourself a little more time is also all these investigations that add nothing but to consolidate your own position and preferably get the opponent off balance. You also buy yourself some time.

Referring to research but not presenting any credible objective documents is another way to end the debate, or not to start it. Research results also differ for what is done with the data. In extensive work, you can select the results that you think benefit your own cause, but this can never give an overall picture of the "*truth*". There are companies that have put in place a system to let anyone present their research in respected forums in order to make money from this. One example was when a German journalist collected some material on the internet and talked about them at a conference where he received applause for his greatness. He had no idea what he was talking about, but he received applause. Just one example of hypocrisy and that everything is just about making big money.

From previously being a subtle message embedded in a movie, like Coca-Cola's early commercial, the commercial has become the most prominent thing today when watching TV.

I don't know what the purpose of the advertising is other than that the creators bring up racist thoughts.

An example is when a black woman and a white man are going to perform some activities and the black woman is portrayed as smart while the white man is portrayed as extremely stupid. It may seem like a funny element to many, but what if you turn it around and let the black woman appear stupid and the white man as smart, well, then it would have gained momentum in the debate.

Then there would be a lot of PK media and politicians who can't stay away from either Twitter/X or their own PK media.

I don't know if the advertisers are aware of their racist messages, which are probably an attempt to show how well integrated immigrants are, it becomes a forced assimilation process that they think the Swede is buying. It is nothing short of provocative and, above all, ridiculous. They may not even be aware of what message they are conveying or if they are, it is very worrying. They have taken on a role in forcing integration on the advice of politicians. They want to feel like nurturing parents for some reason.

It is very instructive and a great asset that we have media that clearly describes how wrong we have done all our lives when, for example, we are going to open a can of tomatoes. It is then that their greatness as a provider of objective information so enlighteningly tells us how to do it according to their own expert knowledge. They often also refer to experts, but it is unclear who these experts are. Maybe it's that they're actually referring to themselves in all their shyness. Their goodness is great that allows us to share in their incredible life wisdom, despite their young age at times.

That they try to be spokespersons for these people who have moved here is nothing but a mockery and a play of the fact that they do not believe that they can help themselves, as if they would be worth less in their eyes and incapable of their own agency. They are simply seen as less knowledgeable. Whether this can be seen by the general public as worrying is difficult to know, but to me it is clear and it smells a bit of racism as well.

When my parents came in 1944 and 1947 respectively, there was no SFI or anything like that. They had to start their lives right away with work and lo and behold, they made it.

There are more immigrants in advertising today, with all kinds of mixes, than natives. The idea is probably that we should be led to believe that they are a well-integrated part of society that has been here for a long time.

Or the advertisement with a sullen Afghan man who patiently and carefully disassembles a package at the recycling station to show how good he is, it is downright ridiculous.

It probably says more about those who created the advertisement than about the recipients.

When I was little and someone teased someone else, that person said - *the one who said it he was it*. In other words, the one who attacked someone else was actually the one who had the strange thoughts that they were trying to transfer to someone else's mouth. In the same way it is today when some politicians and media people accuse someone of being a racist. It is really they themselves who are, it is in their own world of thoughts that these racist words flourish daily.

Those who accuse others of being racists are thus the biggest racists themselves, but legitimize their own racism by transferring it to someone else and at the same time take the right to be racist at someone else's expense and also get recognition from others for this, much like a jester on stage who gets applause for his actions. It is commendable in today's society to accuse someone of racism, then they probably feel a little more comfortable in their own meagre thoughts. It can be a way of seeking community and approval from a group of people they admire and want so much to belong to that they do not hesitate to take advantage of the fear that exists today in society to tell the truth and not to be tainted by their own thoughts. Better then to try to make a penny by selling your own racism but packaged in and at someone else's expense.

Normally, you pay to buy or take part in a service in society, but in the case of advertising, you have to pay not to take part in it.

It's a strange relationship really. Thus, the advertisers know that you don't really want to take part in their advertising but have no choice if you don't pay to be free from it.

Today, advertising is more aggressive than before. An example is when you receive a message on your mobile phone that you are making mistakes, not just one, but three errors when handling your data. You should absolutely not pay for more cloud storage or expand your storage memory and you should not manually delete your photos. No, you should install a program for free that removes duplicates on your device. That it would cost to use the service later is not clear in the first stage – (I don't know if it costs, I haven't tried the service). The fact that the person also sounds very authoritarian and almost screams out the words desperately makes me recoil and think of the 1930s. The idea seems to be to scare the user into correcting their mistakes.

When you save your data today, you can do it with encryptions and passwords. It becomes difficult to access the information that resides in each device.

But if you install the program that the aggressive American voice almost demands you to do, you open up your device (voluntarily) and you are free to read and copy data. Or maybe it's that the program you install turns a blind eye to the content itself and sends it for destruction immediately. That is certainly the case.

You may also pay (if you use the installed software and allow yourself to be robbed) to take part of that information if you then want to search for information via some AI program and your own information happens to appear on the screen.

Is it the desperation to be able to justify your expensively developed AI software that makes you want to be able to expand the content in the AI sphere? It is probably up to everyone to decide for themselves what they want to believe.

The political function that advertising has in society is downright frightening. It takes over more and more of the broadcasts and everyone who is to be supported by it creates a great pressure to make it more comprehensive. There seems to be no end to what people can lower themselves to do to be seen on TV and earn a few bucks. More and more former athletes and actors are taking on any assignment to get some attention and money.

Showing up today in all different types of media and silly TV shows seems to be the only thing that attracts many. It seems to be a manifestation of an insecurity and inadequacy that must be confirmed by others and also make money from. It almost seems like prostitution where the actors can be made to do anything for money. That they are well trained is clear. Swagger and fun and the drive of other people is something that Swedes highly appreciate. But the clear message behind it seems to go unnoticed.

When presenting various sporting events today, the focus seems to have shifted from the football match itself, if we take that as an example.

Before the match is played, a studio of commentators and experts dressed in the latest clothing fashion will discuss and show off.

It starts with up-talk, talk-in-between, interviews, after-talk, down-talk and where these people sit and talk about how good their own effort is. The fact that it is a match to be played becomes of secondary importance, unfortunately it will only be a time when they are not allowed to appear in the box. It may almost be perceived as an insult that we are not allowed to listen and be enraptured by their immense knowledge.

That they also amount to maybe 10+ people to be paid for is another story.

When the TV license became mandatory for everyone in Sweden, this generosity was unleashed in earnest. There is no need for self-criticism of SVT, they have the money anyway and do with it what pleases them.

That we taxpayers are footing the bill is great, they probably think. It was a mistake to let go of the voluntary TV license.

To stand up for your values fully and not be afraid of what others will think is destructive in the long run. What are society's expectations of an old man. When you sit here in your chamber and the political situation is chaotic, then it is difficult to feel joy and meaningfulness. Sitting and being bitter becomes a daily occurrence when darkness gathers and everything feels so uncertain about most things. To join the queue at St. Peter's is perhaps not a bad idea, the day will probably come sooner or later and it can be good to have booked a place in the queue system. Maybe you can get a window table. The question is whether it carries upwards or downwards? Maybe it depends a bit on who you ask about what might be appropriate? Is there a democratic vote or is it a vote that decides. But since we are in Sweden, it will probably be negotiated with the union as well.

That a society can change so drastically that an individual who has been completely uninterested in politics is drawn into politics when the stupidity becomes increasingly clear and bigger and the established politicians do not realize what is happening, then it has gone downhill far more than what at least I and a lot of others are also able to watch without reacting. It should be the case that the established media should ask themselves why so many alternative media are emerging, it can't be that they just grow up because it's fun to spend money and time to let their voice be heard. The fact that two opposite poles are then created that are each other's total extremes and create confusion in society is also something that causes society to be pulled apart more and more. But it may be that a politician can know how to solve problems, but in their eyes the biggest problem then becomes how they can be re-elected after solving the problems.

It is no longer possible to stand on the sidelines and just watch and accept what happens when a society is on its way to its demise. That the signal does not go through at all to the politicians that something is wrong is incomprehensible to me. Are they really that uninterested or is it just cowardice and ignorance that they show and that they hope that someone else will solve the problems without them getting shit under their fingernails.

CENSORSHIP

What exactly is censorship?

In my opinion, this is just a way of preventing a dissenting opinion from being put forward. It has nothing to do with right or wrong, only the desire of an individual or group not to allow a certain sentence to be expressed. If you can also, do it to discredit or smear the person who has this opinion that is in their opinion, deviant, well, then it is your own happiness completely.

MENTAL (UN)HEALTH

What is mental health? Is there any black and white scale that you profess to? Or can it be just about anything where a subjective well-being is experienced as self-evidently different for all people, just like appearance and actions. Is there a template that was created once upon a time that should appear normal and that you are then judged based on by society. What may be one individual's well-being may be another individual's non-well-being.

Do we have the right to put people in different boxes for well-being or should we accept how we all are? What is right and what is wrong. An action based on a subjective feeling can be harmful to one individual but beneficial to another. When does a bad action become bad and when does a good action become good? An action may be performed to reduce one's own guilty conscience and may not be performed to really benefit the recipient of the action. What is such an act worth then? Can one refer to this good deed as a good deed if it is done primarily to justify one's own bad conscience.

If you feel that the society you live in is insane, how do you stand it? Should one join the crowd and allow oneself to be enveloped by this madness or should one fight back? I am doubtful that in the long run we will be able to resist as the pressure from society is too great. Waging this hopeless struggle seems endless and beyond all reason. How is it even possible that politicians do not see what is happening? Are they competent to lead a country with blinders over eyes and ears, that is a recurring question I ask myself and probably others with me. If I were like them, I'd be ashamed of myself. How do they have the nerve to be able to look the voters in the eye?

Is a certain amount of mental illness a healthy reaction to an unhealthy environment? You can feel that things are wrong but can't bring yourself to find a solution to the unhealthy?

How could the rise of Nazism in Germany take place, the great mass was not aware of the danger. Perhaps they, like today's citizens, just went with the flow and did not dare to make their voices heard.

What is the difference between then and now?

THE GOLDEN AGE OF GYM CHAINS

First, we pay big money for food and then we pay big money to burn it. When you consider that there are millions of people who do not have food for the day, the situation becomes a bit strange. The clothing industry also wants its fair share of the pie, offering a large number of fittings, cool fashionable collections that help maintain an inflated self-image. It is also a way to build up one's own defence capability in the event of attacks from a number of potential perpetrators who do not shy away from anything.

What drives so many people to visit different gyms and pay big money when at the same time there are so many other ways to burn calories for free, we even get paid to do it? We do not pay for performing physical work when we perform a job that we are employed to perform.

In the past, you worked and got a dose of physical work that way. Today, you should avoid doing physical work during a work shift, instead you go to a gym to do the same thing. At the gym, heavy lifting is not a problem. The employer may pay for it via health allowance when it is performed at a gym. Taxpayers are also involved in paying for this through tax deductions for the employer for these health-promoting activities. It comes across as a bit comical. Physical work that you are paid to do in your employment is thus considered harmful, but a hard physical workout in a gym is admirable and should be encouraged. There is also something called PT (personal trainer) which of course also costs money. Perhaps an employer, who has the audacity to demand that a worker perform physical work, can hire a PT for each worker so that the worker lifts his goods in a gentle way, if it is the problem that the worker does not lift correctly at his workplace. This would create many new jobs and thus benefit society as a whole. Imagine if, for example, every driver who delivers goods would have a PT in the car who ensures that the lifting is done correctly, there would be many new jobs.

The problem then becomes the customer who is to receive a delivered package that weighs e.g. 29 kilos. If the driver is not allowed to lift more than 28 kg, for example, what should the customer do with the package? The parcel must be taken care of and lifted into the home if it is a private customer.

Perhaps packages over a specified weight should not be delivered to customers as it can have serious consequences for the customer to have to lift these weights. It thus seems that the customer also needs a PT to lift in the right way, which creates additional jobs.

We live in a society with liberal values where everyone is accepted, everyone should be included, no matter what we look like, but still many people want to change their bodies to imitate models. Is this pursuit of perfection really an expression of something else, a way to get rid of frustrations with a society that is not as tolerant as we think.

To then chase the life out of you takes away the thoughts for the moment. If a person feels mentally unwell, the outlet for anger and aggression that a session at the gym can provide can be an alternative to a therapy visit. Both cost some money, but the therapy visit is more expensive. Perhaps an individual's uncertainty about their thoughts and reflections makes it easier to go to a gym and chase the crap out of themselves than to discuss various thoughts and thoughts about the development of society with some fellow human being?

Is this a Swedish way of acting instead of going out on the streets and showing their dissatisfaction? In other countries, you can read that people are going out and protesting more often, but not here to the same extent. Is it a fear of giving vent to your opinions and instead tormenting yourself away for a while during this gym session. There is also a mentality that someone else will fix the problems.

Perhaps they are aware that the police can register them if they go out on the streets and protest and perhaps cage them because they have shown that they are not satisfied with how society has developed? Dealing with one's anxiety about society's decadence may be mitigated by instead tormenting oneself during an expensive gym session to avoid thinking about what society looks like, a society that they can see is something wrong with but do not know, or dare to protest against? Of course, there are big individual differences to why you visit a gym.

I am aware that this is not perceived as politically correct to express, but it is just a thought that pops into my head. The fact that we have freedom of opinion on paper is not the same as that we actually have it. In Sweden, it is just a piece of paper, as in so many other cases. We create papers that no one reads. But to show an image abroad, it can be good to have, even if it has begun to be questioned by more and more countries, they see through the hypocrisy. Perhaps the politicians do not understand this hypocrisy themselves, and what does it say about the quality of our politicians? It will be as more and more people begin to realize, that they are not very knowledgeable as they would have us believe.

SURVIVAL STRATEGIES

The following story was described to me by a psychiatrist working at a Refugee Medical Centre when we studied a course in consultation techniques together. It was the survival strategy of a number of captured soldiers as they were imprisoned in separate dungeons where they could not see each other, only talk to each other. Each evening, one of the groups described in detail how they went to a fancy restaurant in Paris and had a delicious meal. They described the meal in great detail, thus getting a distraction from the situation they were in, and thus being able to look forward to the day when they were free and could enjoy such a meal in real life. It became a driving force for survival that helped them in the moment. This was repeated every day with a new restaurant visit. How many more similar stories are there that have helped people survive. What don't you do to survive, after all, the drive to live is strong and can come up with the most amazing strategies for this survival.

What strategies have I used to survive in Swedish society? Having been born in a country as a stateless person and only at the age of 7 obtaining a citizenship contributed to me feeling alienated and not feeling at home in Sweden. What would my life have been like if my parents hadn't been forced to leave Estonia during the Soviet Union's annexation of their country? The exile that both my parents went into and which was not voluntary, it leaves its mark even if they have been well hidden. The difficulty for me to find an identity that has existed has not been easy to put into words before.

POLITICAL DRIVING FORCES

What drives a politician to become a politician? Is it a way to impose their own worldview on another person that can be more or less distorted or healthy? But as a politician, you get paid to present and try to convince another person that your own worldview is correct. Could there be mental illness behind such thoughts? Some kind of hubris or superhuman feeling?

Isn't history also full of such people who have gradually been portrayed as evil, sick but who just for the moment have been considered brilliant and much loved by a large crowd. Or have they, based on a position of strength, only been able to manipulate the large mass without the mass having the power, courage or will to challenge the person. Is man basically just an obedient sheep who allows himself to be led, sometimes to the end and death of the world? Or does man assume that all people are good and cannot think that anyone wants to hurt them. This naivety is certainly different in different cultures as well. If you

187

make a population sufficiently uncertain, you can control its population easily with small means, perhaps through small alms of some kind.

I am eternally grateful that I have always been outside the machinations and hypocrisy of politics. I have always found it disgusting to have to buy a number of arguments for a position that has as many arguments for as against.

Perhaps it is mostly a community you join when you become a member of a political party, in the same way that you can become a member of a cult to seek out like-minded people. You surround yourself with a palisade like Armor with which you feel protected by your peers. If you are a member of a sect or political party, you are free to express racist views as well, then it counts as clean, even something grand. You just project your own inherent racism onto a political opponent and voila, you are embraced by your own party's sympathies for their incredible wisdom. You only seek political points at the expense of an opponent.

What drives a politician to become a politician? If a person outside the game of political hypocrisy expresses a similar thought to an established politician, well, then that person is a racist.

Have people's thinking really changed over the years or is it not the same questions and thoughts over the centuries that constantly affect us, both large and small?

A fundamental factor is that we humans cannot live together in peace and that you cannot politically decide that people should do if everything is to end well.

Even if politicians with all good intentions try to look beyond people's differences, they exist.

Haven't all wars through the centuries shown this in a clear way, why else have people tormented each other when they don't have the same religion, for example? I have not read anywhere that the different sides during a war caused by religious differences would call each other racists. Despite the fact that they do not accept their opponent's opinions. It's a bit strange.

Is it personal gain in the end that determines this? Or is it the people (lobbyists) who figure in the vicinity of politics to press on about their particular interests. It is not uncommon to read about politicians who have tried to gain their own gain, sometimes against established regulations. They have then just "forgotten" to announce or do something that they should have done. Maybe this only applies if they are caught with their fingers in the jam jar.

That so many people with great power without knowledge can be allowed to destroy so much without having to take responsibility for it and also not have insight into this themselves is a mystery to me.

Wanting to do something is more important than being able to do it well, whatever the cost, as long as you have the right colour on your party book. This is despite the fact that we read daily about how a nation that has had such a system now violates another nation. A nation that many praised in the past but today do not accept, other than their previous ideology.

WHAT IS HAPPINESS

What would a happy life have been like? It's a bit far-fetched to think back and fill in the broken pieces with what can be perceived as happiness. What appears to be happiness can also be misfortune disguised in pink shimmer. We humans in Sweden have a stubborn ability not to show what we deep down feel, the outward appearance is the important thing. Perhaps that is why we are seen as hypocrites by more and more countries. We think we are so good, but we live extremely strongly controlled by the state without reacting to it. Swedish society tears families apart and takes over the individual, enticing with benefits and benefits that are ultimately just borrowed money, a kind of prostitution. If the state opens its subsidy tap in exchange for oppressing the people, the individual is satisfied.

It is strange that more people do not see through this smokescreen that the state is putting out. There is always a bill to be paid in the end. Where that bill ends up, you don't have to be an Einstein to understand, it ends up in the lap of the taxpayers, of course. This is to maintain a power to be able to monitor and oppress the ordinary citizen. How does a Swede in international comparison really stand intellectually? Better or worse or maybe equivalent? If you look at the politicians we have today, I become doubtful as they do not seem to have Sweden's best interests in mind, but more how to avoid that reality is described.

Can it really continue in the same way or will the lies be revealed at some point and what will happen then. Will it then be the old usual that now we should not look backwards but forwards and see the possibilities instead. At the same time, it is usually said that we should learn from the mistakes, but when it comes down to it, we do not want that. If this is not hypocrisy, I do not know what is. This is what makes it so difficult to trust our politicians, they have no idea how things are connected, something that they should have if they are to sit and govern the country. Once again, the question of the driving force comes to the fore among the politicians, what do they really want with their power? Do they understand their role themselves or is it only the allure of being in the spotlight as a narcissist that is important to them, regardless of whether they know something or not?

PAIN

When pain takes over life, then the very meaning of life has changed from being something to enjoy to something to put up with. To be followed day in and day out by this pain breaks down what little meaning is left and doubts accumulate. The pain also eats away at mood and willingness to seek social contacts, and loneliness increases. It becomes a negative spiral that only goes downwards. You also don't want to tell those around you that you have this constant pain and maybe be seen as a weakling. Perhaps this is why the thoughts arise that you like the animals withdraw and avoid contact and thus possible inconvenience to the surroundings. Not being a burden on anyone is a fundamental weakness that exists in some people's inner selves and it can certainly be perceived by others as just the opposite, an arrogance not to seek contact.

To feel contempt for both life and death becomes a strange ambivalent feeling that tastes both sour, sweet, salty and bitter at the same time.

A contempt that is characterized by a feeling of having been deceived by what life could provide but still not served. A self-defeating will to fit in and to believe that those around you are sincere when it has always been about the lisping game of hypocrisy behind the scenes. The falsehood that is the very foundation of society and which, if mastered, rewards both wealth and success. Is this really how a society should work? Is there no better way to keep a society together? Is man really just a primitive predator who has glued on a layer of social varnish that can be different thicknesses for different individuals. If you scratch the surface a little, a selfish little bastard appears there as a letter in the mail.

THE HEALING POWER OF MUSIC

That music can make a person feel good is nothing new, but what is it that makes you feel better? Different situations are handled by different types of music, lively, thoughtful, sad or happy.

The fact that we appreciate music in different ways and also how it is performed is a basis for the fact that there is countless equipment to play music on as a complement to live gigs. Some want a slightly lighter character while others want a slightly duller character. I usually think of it as us wanting to have different centres of gravity in the soundscape. Personally, I like a lower centre of gravity with a slightly duller character. Music becomes a way to escape the hypocrisy of life, in the same way that genealogy can take away from thinking about the present.

LIFE AS A PINBALL MACHINE

That life can feel like a pinball machine is perhaps not so strange. The bullet that is allowed to be the driving force to influence life is pushed around by circumstances that can be difficult to grasp at a quick glance. It can also hurt sometimes when someone who uses the tools available to move the ball into the game bets with extra full force to get the ball as far into the game as possible and thus collect a number of points to maybe also get a free game and extend the game, or the suffering that it can mean to whirl around the playing field of life seemingly uncontrollably. But is it uncontrolled or random, perhaps there is an inherent plan that is executed via these bullets? We get a number of balls that we have to do as much as possible with and sometimes we can get one or two extra balls if we have been good.

That we play on different playing fields becomes extra clear when we see the different conditions that are presented to us at the start and

192

changing playing fields is not possible in the easiest team either, it can require both finesse and cunning and maybe a little more sometimes, as we all seek a more equipped playing field with more opportunities to acquire bonuses and rewards in the form of extra points. Some playing fields are more richly decorated from the start than others and it will be our lot to stay on that court and make the best of it.

Can you then not change the playing field becomes a question that arises and sure, some try and can even succeed with it, but most of us stay on the one that has been assigned to us. Out of convenience of some and inability of others, the reasons can vary. Some find themselves in their situation while others may do anything to switch to one that they see as more attractive but which in the end may not be so attractive when trying to learn its game. Some may remove the thin transparent glass that prevents us from influencing the game, while some tinker with the playing field and some find themselves looking at everything through the glass. Is there anything that prohibits someone from removing the glass and thus being able to keep the ball in play for longer?

We have probably all been dazzled by gold in sunshine. If you are too violent in the game, the built-in protection also steps in and closes down the game and you have lost. TILT! If you look at different time perspectives when you are on a playing field, the result will be different.

If you look at a perspective over a decade, it may seem important what you do, but if you increase the time perspective to, say, a century, the importance of what we as individuals do decreases and if you look at a millennium, it is completely forgotten for most of us, only a few individuals get stuck in the historical perspective. How long can we manage to keep the historical perspective up to date? Some look at life only here and now, something that makes for a more pleasant journey on the playing field, while others who try to see the horizon find it more difficult. If you try to look too far, it creates problems too. The day we no longer wander around the playing field, time stops or is still there, and then only for those who are left on the playing field.

Isn't time just a social construct that we humans have created to have something to hang our lives on in order to have a common reference to work around? Is it so important when everything ends one day for all of us and new individuals are added who play on their own playing fields. Creating your own playing fields will probably be easier in the future as reality can be created by anyone in imagination and artificial intelligence. Perhaps the demands to conform to common values will also cease, the liberal, anarchist social order places less and less demand on the individual and thus everything will collapse like a house of cards one day?

DENIAL

How can you live in a denial for a whole life of not daring to express your will but only seek in your surroundings what you think is best for the moment? Like an opportunist or chameleon, trying to blend in with his surroundings. To walk around with an insecurity that so desperately manifests itself in a theft or borrowing of opinions in an environment that shapes a person into a shapeless package. But being a pragmatist has its points in this context.

How many people actually live their lives on their own terms?

Perhaps far fewer than one might think. What does it mean to not live your life on your own terms? Is it life itself that takes us in different directions and we just follow along as passive servants or can we influence the direction to some extent or even fully? It must probably be seen as being completely individual and how well we have been equipped to take advantage of life's opportunities and to deal with its pinches and setbacks. Some learn it early from home while others learn it in life's hard school and how to manage to make life something so tolerable and where some never learn this but have to fend off the obstacles that arise more or less in panic.

When the feeling of wanting to crawl into a world with an enveloping shell arises in order to relax, it is to be able to try to find one's inner core of harmony. In the same way as refraining from seeking out your old friends or if it is the case that the old friends choose not to see you, perhaps by sending signals about wanting to be left alone.

To constantly try to give the appearance of being satisfied with life and to seem busy and to be involved in society, when in fact you are sitting alone and depressed in your room is a difficult art that can only be refined through years of practice.

That you don't want to appear as a failed individual but try to show that you are in the game of life is not so remarkable in itself. But it certainly shines through the veil of obscure participation that they are trying to spread around. Who wants to voluntarily talk about being alone and lost in life. It would seem like you're weird and odd and you don't want that voluntarily, do you?

At the same time, you don't want to as it can be revealed that you are a very lonely person who is just waiting for death's merciless or merciful embrace. The shame of these cloudy thoughts can run like a red thread through life. Life may not have turned out as expected, something that many can probably recognize. The energy that previously existed to keep going can be on the wane and the flame slowly but inexorably fades. It is a process that can no longer be reversed, but one must calmly accept it as a last outpost before death. What awaits on the other side really, it's not without getting curious. The pain as a constant companion will hopefully disappear and you may finally get peace in body and soul.

MORAL COMPASS

Having a strong inner moral compass that cannot be followed out in society can play many tricks on us in life. Trying to follow this compass can sometimes be perceived as doing exactly the opposite just because you can't fit into the lying world you live in. Hypocrisy is praised as social competence when it is really just a fear that one frantically tries to overcome by embracing what other people in their eyes praiseworthy people do in the belief that they have the right opinions and actions.

When a majority of a society's citizens embrace this and it is wrong, it takes odd root in society and poisons its soul. A deeply inherited sense of right and wrong can backfire as just the opposite when you try to hold against its values. The only one who has to pay the price for this is the one who has these values and an existence outside the inner circle of the established society is a fact. Being in society and trying to integrate into it is one thing and another to succeed with your intentions. The desire for one or the other is also a factor to consider.

A JOURNEY INWARDS

To journey into oneself and try to understand one's own thoughts, feelings and actions is an endless process that one must try not to get stuck in but still search with light and lantern if curiosity arises. Some people probably think that it is a waste of time and effort and that can be the case, but it can also be interesting to explore this part if you keep a little distance from the search. Society today is designed so that it spins faster and faster and the question is to what use? Is the intention to thereby limit the individual's opportunities to analyse and question the political decisions that we believe are made on rational grounds, but which may just be a seamstress of vague and populist opinions that will be overplayed in a couple of months?

It is as if you want to cover up real problems by rushing past them. Everything becomes like a dizzying dance with dizziness as a result, and thus the field of vision is limited. If you can also feed the population with more financial resources, the common man will soon forget about the real problems in society and drug himself with these financial means, which are probably just borrowed money, and those who have stopped and thought about the state of things in society are seen as conspiracy theorists or whiners.

Most likely, the answer will one day be revealed and then those responsible will say why didn't you stop us and then they will get away. Turning the coat inside out when new times are approaching is not the first time in world history. There was a time when politicians were considered knowledgeable and wise people, but that image has today changed to exactly the opposite.

Perhaps it has always been the same way, but in today's society it is easier to expose the political corruption that exists in Sweden as well. What is it that drives a politician to become a politician, is it to be able to live on taxpayers' money and not have to add anything but just eat from the cake? When politicians stop running on nitrous oxide and come down to earth, maybe there is hope.

THE FLAME OF LIFE

When the flame of life is lit, you have no idea how long it will shine. It can go out early and it can shine for a long time. Maybe it's lucky that you don't know how long it shines, how would you plan your life based on that knowledge? Is the uncertainty itself perhaps the price you have to pay to get your flame lit? One should focus away from the very fact that one has a measured time that is different for all people. Some succeed in doing so, and others carry this knowledge visibly.

When you get older and you sit alone and sad and wonder what the meaning of the flame of life is, it is difficult to realize that you have received a gift when your flame has been lit. But that is not enough to ignore the pain that can be in the soul. Nothing may feel meaningful other than the knowledge and hope that one's offspring are doing well and one's own role fades away in the game of life. A game that as you get older becomes more and more obvious and the hypocrisy that society exhibits. That there should be such a thing as honour and morality today is unfortunately not true, it has been washed away a long time ago. For whom do you live your life?

Today, with the liberal attitude to the way of life, one should not make any demands on the citizens, only one's own loss counts, the more deviant (what is deviant can be difficult to define), the more celebrated it is. It seems that the most extreme is the one that is appreciated the most. From being a country that we previously called *"lagom"*, Sweden has now become the country of extremes in many respects. Our politicians who are supposed to protect their citizens' money also compete in being extreme, but I hope that citizens will wake up at some point and realize what is about to happen.

Who or what decides how long the flame should burn? The genetic code is a factor, but is it then chance (illness and accidents can also influence) that determines or how the individual lives his or her life or has been brought up? Can a person live a whole life without loving or being loved? Do you have to have been loved as a child to be able to give love as an adult? How else do you know what that means. You cannot miss something you do not know exists, and is it then a way to protect yourself from painful insights. If you had known what you were missing and not experienced it, how do you react. Ignorance of one's situation can be good as a protective shell around oneself. How do you know what love is?

For some, the flame is just the transport distance that remains of life, the flame has already begun to burn the hand that holds it. Maybe you don't have to feel fear, but just a kind of anticipation of what will happen after the flame is extinguished. Shame may have characterized life and permeated everything a person has done. Why did it turn out like this, it's a question that many people may have asked themselves many times without having received an answer to. Perhaps you are not supposed to get answers to all your questions.

Is it mostly a coincidence that determines where the flame is lit, in what environment. Some have a nice upbringing and others don't. But as a child, you are not aware of anything other than the environment you actually grow up in. Of course, you can see that some others seem to be doing well, but you don't focus on the fact that there are different conditions for all people. You see it from the child's perspective and not like after a whole life based on an overview that you didn't have as a child. It should not be confused with self-pity, but rather seen as a comparison after a number of years out in the merry-go-round of society.

THE CYCLE OF THE SOUL

Is the soul something that just lives on in its own cycle regardless of the body it is currently in? When the body dies it is said that the soul lives on and some people even claim to be able to get in touch with these souls later. Whether this is true or not, I cannot decide, but I can allow myself to think a bit about it. Something that is popular in Sweden is the programs where mediums claim to get in touch with spirits who have not really found peace and these mediums then help these poor souls over to the right side, the side of the dead, where they can find peace.

There are religions that see the soul as part of a cyclical process where one can be reborn in a later life in another form, animal or human. The primary thing would be the soul and not a perhaps frail bodily package. Is this what drives some people on in life, a hope of later having a better life on earth? Since all people have different living conditions and not the same conditions as are sometimes claimed, life becomes difficult in different ways. A common thing is that we will all die once, that is inevitable. But what drives people to cope with life when it is difficult? It may seem like a shortcut to a better next life to end the existing life prematurely in order to perhaps have a better life sooner. But perhaps it is the fear of crossing the border that prevents people in general from coming to their senses, even though a large number of people do not hesitate to end their lives prematurely.

Perhaps there is also an uncertainty about a next possibly better life?

Not to go around thinking all our lives that we are just waiting to die is a matter of course. When we get sick, we can be reminded of our mortality and then a strong will to live on takes hold of us and we let go of the thoughts of an approaching death. Maybe it's good to be reminded sometimes. What does a cycle look like for our souls? When a human being is born, is this person provided with a soul that is in a layer some-where and that by chance would fit the newborn?

Or is there a match by someone who creates a configuration based on previously related souls? Who could this configuration manager be? Is that what we call God? God is a super configurator who has a number of helpers who do the practical work. When a soul leaves a body, does it return to a central warehouse to later be matched in a new individual? How long can a soul exist? Forever maybe. When a soul is given a new body to travel in, is it so that it will evolve further and eventually achieve some kind of nirvana? Is this what determines the differences in the people that the souls that are in their bodies have made different numbers of journeys to Earth and thus evolved differently in the pursuit of the ultimate level, a level that everyone reaches in the end?

The body becomes only like a container that serves the soul for a short time. If we just borrow a number of recycled cells that form a body with a number of organs that can then be implemented with a soul from the warehouse. Some people say that they can identify with previous exist-ences, what is usually called "*déjà vu*", that they recognize themselves and that they feel that they have lived in a previously familiar time. Maybe you have been given a soul that you have had in a previous life on earth.

Can the soul also really affect how long it wants to stay in the body? If it is dissatisfied, it can then speed up the process to be placed in a new and perhaps more exciting body. Do different souls seek different levels of adventure? Some don't need much at all, while others need lots of adventure. But in order not to constantly worry about your impending death, there may be built-in barriers within us that disconnect from these thoughts.

Or if it is only all the positive things that are expected of us that make the positive thoughts prioritize over the negative ones? A positive balance weighs more than a negative one, at least for some. Dealing with these thoughts is also done in different ways by different people. Some are better at it than others, while some fall into a constant pondering over the issue. Do we share in our destinies or do we just go along when the soul enters a body on earth?

CULTURE

Many people together with me may ask themselves what culture is. Is it something that you can just casually put on or is there some deeper meaning to the concept. As a concept, it is something arbitrary that defines itself according to orientation and background.

I often think I see signs that people are only smearing a superficial layer of culture to blend into a world they long for. Others have a more inner form of expression of culture that manifests itself in a more genuine embodiment.

Should culture only tickle the surface a little or should it set in motion processes from the depths of one's soul?

It is usually possible to see who is just rubbing shoulders in the goodness of culture as one perceives it to be. Belonging to a cultural elite is for some the same thing as belonging to a football club is for others. But if you worship culture, you assume that you are seen as more intellectual and therefore more important. Otherwise, the risk is that you can be seen as just an uneducated jerk or downright stupid.

Others can clearly see that it is something more heartfelt that comes from within and pours out like a volcanic eruption and not as a smeared layer of varnish or eyeshadow that others strive for, preferably with a glass of wine in their hand where the little finger stands straight up in attention.

To liken man to a predator; with a layer of varnish that can be easily scraped off, even if some have a slightly thicker layer that needs to be processed, it is not a completely unwarranted analogy in my eyes.

MATH PROBLEM

Pelle and Fatima have a test in mathematics with the following question:

Lisa puts 2 apples in a box and Mohammad puts 2 apples in the same box; how many apples are there in the box?

Pelle replies that there are 4 apples in the box and Fatima replies that there are 5 apples in the box.

Who is right?

According to the multiplication table that Pelle has been struggling with, Pelle is right, but Fatima thinks it is, or thinks it looks like 5.

How can you prove who is right about Pelle and Fatima?

The fact that we have learned from old habit that 2 plus 2 equals 4 does not necessarily mean that it is right. If someone also gets sad or angry because 2 plus 2 doesn't become 5, then another aspect of the problem is added.

The teacher agrees with both so there is no fight, but Pelle gets sad and goes home to his mother and cries and explains why he is sad. The mother then asks the teacher why Pelle's answer is not the only correct one, to which the teacher replies that it is not possible to determine the correct answer, there will be the least problem with both getting it right.

Maybe it's not important that the answer is right?

The issue would have to be raised to the Riksdag so that our wise elected politicians can decide the issue. Perhaps, however, the issue first needs to be investigated more and thus sent out for consultation to a number of different wise bodies.

If all referral bodies, then come to the conclusion that there are 5 apples in the box and that the Riksdag unanimously passes this, the work remains to convince little Pelle that he was wrong to think that there were 4 apples in the box. It may be a tough time for Pelle, but Fatima is happy that she was right.

Pelle, Mohammad, Lisa and Fatima are actually called something else.

SUMMARY

Despite all the attempts I've made, I haven't been able to get an answer to *when the chickens pee* and it's starting to feel like the answer *never!* And that it may not have been the intention that I would find the answers I was looking for, despite all the different tracks I have followed. However, it has given me some insights and answers to questions that I did not expect to get, but I have not been able to get the most important answers. The labyrinth I have navigated through has not fully revealed the ways out that could give me all my answers.

The answers I hoped to get to my questions by searching on roads outside the direct roads via parents' and relatives' information could not help me other than that I had gained a lot more general knowledge about my relatives, but not the closest ones.

DNA tests have given me new knowledge about both distant and closer relatives, but I have not found any direct genetic connection to my grandfather other than through documentation other than birth certificates.

I also tried a trace I had about the Brüsewitz family and the legend that they would have lost their property.

I read up on the nobility in general to see if I could find any clues there, the only concrete thing was that I could see that it was possible to lose one's title and property and also a couple of examples I found that I have mentioned here. What the legend of the Brüsewitz family interpreted as the loss of title may have been the loss of military rank.

That there have been families who have lost their nobility, it is obvious, but then it has been about individuals who have been affected, not the whole family. I have also included an example of how the right birth was important. Even participation in the Dekabrist rebellion could mean losing one's property, as in the case of Prince Sergei Volkonsky. Did the Brüsewitz family have any connection to this rebellion through Hermann's father? I have also shown connections to some of the main characters in the Dekabrist rebellion. A genetic link to a place of exile in Siberia has also been shown to a male relative.

Another approach was to try to find clues to the family's origins through the godparents of the Brüsewitz family's children and possibly be able to confirm or refute the legend that has existed in the family. It did not provide any concrete evidence either for or against the legend being true.

I also got into a helicopter and flew slowly over the European landscape to look for tracks from above, but could see that I couldn't find any that I could confirm. The helicopter view that was advocated a number of years ago when you wanted to have some perspective on life did not give me the expected results. Maybe I need to clarify that it was not a physical helicopter. But it was a bit like trying to fly with borrowed feathers.

It is clear that the nobility as a social class had a large number of privileges, but they also had a responsibility that was used by many with care for their subjects.

Unfortunately, the new nobility that the politicians represent do not have the same care for their subjects, who have also chosen them to represent their interests.

I have also tried to connect the family to the von Brüsewitz family without finding any connection even though there is a track I would like to drill a little more into, namely a track to Lubainen in Poland, southeast of the city of Olsztyn.

Some random links, albeit vague, have been found between people who have been in the environment around the family. Little did I know that when I sat in a classroom at Realskolan in Norrköping in the 1960s, sitting next to a classmate, as it has now turned out, that we have a somewhat unexpected connection to each other via Russia. But if you put it harder, we are all related to each other if we search the databases.

By what right do I present my thoughts here? Am I entitled to it? The obvious answer is, of course, that I am no righter than anyone else. Still, I do. Is it perhaps a general rebellion in a crazy world? Or maybe it's the lack of answers from when I was a child that has driven me and subconsciously brought out the thoughts that have popped up. The reception the refugees received after WWII differs markedly from today's undemanding immigration. At that time, there were demands that refugees should contribute to their livelihoods and not be a burden on society, something that has changed today if you follow the debate. At that time, immigrants were seen as capable of handling their situation without either SFI (Swedish for Immigrants) or benefits. How do you view today's immigrants from the politicians' perspective? Are they less competent or talented as human beings or why are they not given responsibility for their livelihood? Is it racist to demand this. If that's the case, then my parents and everyone else who came then must have been subjected to racism. Perhaps a truth commission should be appointed so that today's politicians can explain why the view differs so much between immigrants' skills then and now. The humility and gratitude that existed then is completely absent today. Even we children who were born in this country felt gratitude.

I have tried to fill in the void that my childhood offered and that may be why I have never felt fully involved in society. Maybe that's also an explanation for why I haven't been able to bring myself to create the life I originally wanted. It has become a concoction of different solutions, a pragmatism, all the time to parry and adapt the situations that have arisen.

I threw away my future when I fled from medical school at Karolinska after a semester.

There were so many other things around me and there was never any time to fully engage in my studies, I was not present mentally. Instead, I jumped on a couple of other educations, psychology and the Technical University of Stockholm, but I had the same uncommitted efforts there. I ended up moving back to Norrköping and eventually studying for a Master's degree in Cognitive Science in Linköping.

The inner void that has always existed inside me could not be filled, but it gave me something anyway. Was it that I had no chance of creating the life I wanted from the beginning?

There were too many secrets around me and that I also created my own and this pawing on tiptoe and not taking up space shaped my life thoroughly. The fear of revealing my thoughts was constantly there. I had learned by observing my father not to show what I was thinking. Maybe I would have been a good poker player?

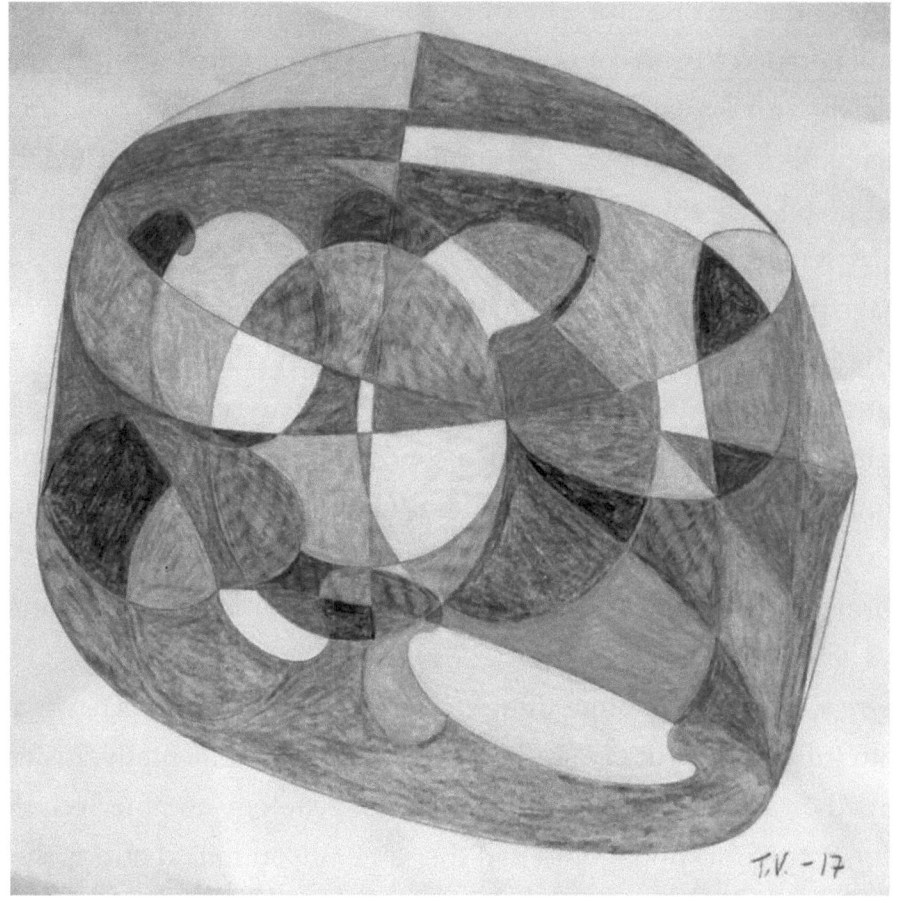

The complex cocoon of life

There is a small unfilled area left in the cocoon that I don't know what it will be filled with. But the most likely scenario is that someone else will have to fill it in for me.

The fact that I have since given a whole lot of different explanations for why things in my life turned out the way they did has felt a bit false and not really true. But I have tried to be pragmatic in these contexts as well when I have given explanations for various events in life, like a pinball machine.

So, when I couldn't find the answers, I was hoping for fully, a number of thoughts in other directions popped up in my head, sometimes suspicious and they could scare me a lot. It has been a balancing act between letting out thoughts that can be perceived as bothersome and describing a reality that can also be questioned and condemned by some.

My sister's comments may say a lot about me that I haven't thought about before:

My task was probably responsibility, especially over you. You had so much going on for you and I had to run and chase after you everywhere. Probably shaped me as a big sister.

The fact that there is only 1 year between us and that we grew up as key children can also be a small explanation for the disorientation. We got to explore life on our own when we were little. You explored the world in your own way and the consequences I had to take as a big sister sometimes.

When our parents came to Sweden and were well received, they did not want to be a burden on society. Living on benefits when they were fully able to work was not on their map. They considered it shameful. Society judged them as competent to provide for their own livelihoods and not as some less knowledgeable individuals who could not take care of themselves. I also don't know what grants were available at that time.

Maybe that's why my sister got a key and thus a responsibility for me too. You can see that my sister early took care of me literally, but I don't know if I seem to appreciate it. I was busy exploring the world in my own way. Maybe I've been doing it all my life.

My sister Virve and I in 1953

Our brother Niklas who is 16 years younger than I am grew up when we were already flown out or about to move away from home, he did not experience our early upbringing.

Being key children was probably the price we children had to pay for their eagerness to enter the labour market and repay the favour they considered it to be to be well received by society as refugees in a difficult time.

This book may be seen as a memory to a father I never got to knew

Maybe Fyodor Dostoyevsky was right.

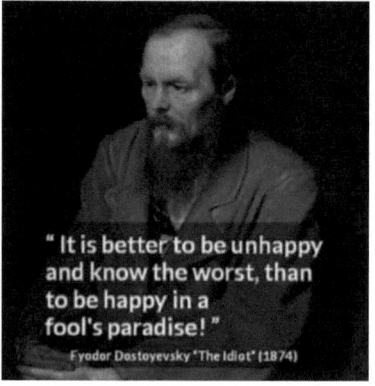

Fyodor Dostoyevsky

Fyodor Dostoyevsky is your third cousin once removed's wife's brother's wife's third cousin once removed's husband.

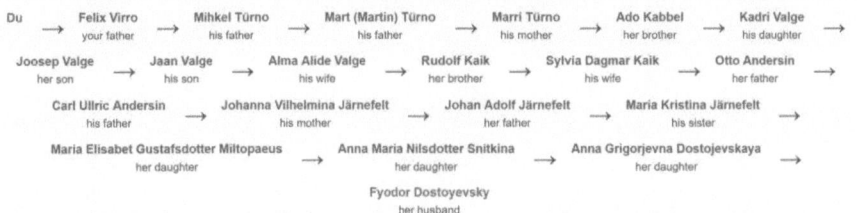

Du → Felix Virro *your father* → Mihkel Türno *his father* → Mart (Martin) Türno *his father* → Marri Türno *his mother* → Ado Kabbel *her brother* → Kadri Valge *his daughter* →

Joosep Valge *her son* → Jaan Valge *his son* → Alma Alide Valge *his wife* → Rudolf Kaik *her brother* → Sylvia Dagmar Kaik *his wife* → Otto Andersin *her father* →

Carl Ullric Andersin *his father* → Johanna Vilhelmina Järnefelt *his mother* → Johan Adolf Järnefelt *her father* → Maria Kristina Järnefelt *his sister* →

Maria Elisabet Gustafsdotter Miltopaeus *her daughter* → Anna Maria Nilsdotter Snitkina *her daughter* → Anna Grigorjevna Dostojevskaya *her daughter* →

Fyodor Dostoyevsky *her husband*

The remains of a life